Draw Me Nearer

by Sharon Eisenberg Farrer

Draw Me Nearer, Sharon Eisenberg Farrer
Willowbranch Publishers
ISBN: 979-8-9904939-0-2

Cover design by Hannah Linder Designs
Interior design by atritex.com

Available in print from your local bookstore, online, or from the publisher.

Library of Congress Cataloging-in-Publication Data
Farrer, Sharon Eisenberg.
Draw Me Nearer / Sharon Eisenberg Farrer, 1st ed.
Printed in the United States of America

Table of Contents

Dedication

I dedicate this book to the women whose lives have inspired and challenged me to seek hard after God in all of my ways that I might know Him as I am known by Him. Your stories are woven through my life and the pages of my writing. The investment you have made in me has inspired me to pour out my life in turn for other women through, Draw Me Nearer.

I dedicate this book also to my pastor, shepherd, brother and Friend

Charles (Charlie) Averett Stakely IV.

1959-2023

Thanks to

God, for answering my prayers over what I was to do with the words He has given to me. Thank you for teaching me to follow You in newfound obedience and service to my sisters in Christ and beyond.

My husband Rodney, who reminds me every day that following God's purpose for my life is all I ever need to do. You've shown me that with your love and support, I can reach beyond the limits I see. Thank you for being Jesus to me and the voice of truth.

Suzanne who was able to take the baby, the first manuscript, and pluck it apart with her mighty pen while responding from her mind and heart. Her investment in this book goes beyond a dollar amount. She can be found in the pages if you look closely.

Look Susie, the baby is finally here.

Diane B, thank you for teaching we younger women, who followed behind you, the value of God's Word and hiding it in our hearts. I'm forever indebted to you for what you've added to my life. Thank you for raising the banner high and teaching me to do the same.

Kim, Rebecca, Winter, and Hollie for taking on the task of reading my manuscript and giving me such beneficial feedback filled with truth and grace. Each of you laid something down to pick this up and I will forever be grateful that you were willing to take my hand and meet the task set before me.

My prayer warriors, who have encouraged me to press on and press into the task placed before me in writing this book according to God's call. Your vital prayers have been realized as you hold this book. Thank you for reminding me of that one woman waiting for this book to be written. You have given me the strength to finish well. Thank you for giving.

He First Loved Me

"This is love: not that we loved God, but that he loved us and sent his Son as an atoning sacrifice for our sins."

1 John 4:10 NIV, ESV, NKJV

Have you known what it is to suffer a great loss? The kind where the hurt seems to be a bottomless pit? Nothing will fix it, fill it, soothe it, stop it, or even slow it down. I find that these words are way more familiar than I'd like to admit. I'm well acquainted with all of the above. I can say now that I'm confident God had a purpose in the hard places of my personal experiences, but I did not have that perspective at the time.

Over fifteen years ago, I watched someone whom I loved very deeply go through a horrible, unexpected loss. Through her experience, I watched her lose her way. Her plumb line was gone, and she rapidly lost her footing. I watched her wrestle, and I did all I could think of to come alongside, console, provide, and protect her from further pain. Yet, the path continued to weave its way, bringing destruction and further devastation. In the process of it all, I realized that this one whom I loved had distanced herself from me, from that which was familiar. I began a prayer journey over this loved one as I'd never ventured before. I literally spent years praying and seeking a bridge to close the gap but to no avail. I asked myself all of the tough questions: Has God forgotten me? Have I revealed what a failure I am?

Did I do enough? Was I destined to live in wonder over what had transpired and question God forever?

There were times when she came back into my space but never stayed. I continued to wonder, would she ever know peace? I then faced four years in which I lost my mom and my dad. I questioned in my own heart: will I forever be losing people whom I love? At that point, it seemed a fair question. The thought was too large for my head and my heart. It was then that I found a deeper determination in prayer. I had no idea, honestly, whether I'd ever be free to love this person again. The thought was excruciating, and I had to do something with the love and pain. I chose to pray that God would not let her go and that He would bring her back to Himself even if she never returned to me. What drove this prayer? It was the realization of what I already knew was true: God loved her as He loved me. If she turned back to God, then I knew that the love of God could fill her, and perhaps, just maybe, she would return for me to love her.

Several times along this long path, God prompted me to reach out even though I knew there would be no response. I did it. I made sure that I spoke the truth from my heart and simply told her that I loved her and missed her. Then, I prayed once more. There was grieving and letting go through those four years, but I never stopped praying or reaching. And then, one day, it happened. I reached out to her, and she responded. We agreed upon a time to meet with one another. Many times, I'd wept at the thought of this experience because I felt I'd forgotten what she even looked like.

After a few attempts and a sense of fear and doubt, I received a text from her. She asked if we could get together "that day." Well, of course, there was only one answer. I was filthy from cleaning the house all morning. To make things even more exciting I had a deliveryman coming to install a washer and dryer that afternoon. I said, yes, come over to my house. I got to see her, touch her, talk to her, and hear what was in her heart. She then asked me if I was ready to be a grandmother again. You guessed it, this is one of my daughters.

One visit grew into several great visits and phone conversations. I was in complete awe of the power of God displayed in His choosing to answer my prayers in this beautiful way. I became acutely aware of what having a heart of gratitude and humility looked like. I knew I could never have caused this to happen and that I'd fully given it to God. He clearly was not done.

Perhaps you have a difficult obstacle that you have been facing for what seems like way too long. Let me be the first to tell you God is not done. There's a song I love that has the phrase, "It ain't over till I say it's over, and I say that it ain't over yet." I take these words seriously as I reflect on God's position and power over every aspect of life.

Throughout the process and this period, there were times I stumbled under the weight of it all. There were days I felt that God was still working, and there were days I wondered. But how I felt did not drive my prayers. My love for God and hope in His power and His Word was what continually drove me. The most important thing that I could cling to was the fact that God loved me first. My desire for change came from the fact that He loved me and gave everything for me. I knew that I needed to take Him at His word and trust that His love would see me safely to the other side of this situation, whatever that may look like.

In scripture, God repeatedly tells us not to give up on what we have been given to do and not to hang our hope on outcomes. He alone will be our reward. This season of suffering was for my growth in seeing God as He is and seeing His power working on my behalf. Many times, we go through places where we feel like we are lost and in a deep, dark forest. But this is when we can choose to tell ourselves the truth that has been given to us in God's Word.

I am still in awe of this intimate Father I serve and need daily. Take your cares to Him and ask Him for exactly what you desire. Then, stay at the foot of that cross and continue to trust His love and faithfulness. He is listening, and He will answer in His own time. You are not alone. Sometimes, the answer will not be what you were asking for, which is of God's choosing too. If you find that He is silent, then rest assured that He is still working. He hears your prayers. Remember, our primary prayer to Him is that His will be done. That may mean surrendering our will to His better way.

We must remind ourselves daily that despite how we feel, God is working on our behalf. Only that which is on the solid Rock cannot be moved. So, fix your eyes on His love for us and depend on it to lead you to the end of the journey. He is our God, whom we can always trust.

Dear God,

I can't say that I fully understand Your love for me in that You sent Jesus to suffer and die for me. And yet I know that I can trust Your love beyond myself. My understanding can never explain fully Your heart or mind. I thank You that when I can't see or feel You, I can choose to acknowledge and claim Your Word and its truths. You love me. Thank You for all that You did for me at the cross of Christ and for enabling me to love as You do. I know You hear my prayers. Make me patient to wait on You as You accomplish all of Your holy will in me.

Amen.

Proverbs 3:5 Isaiah 26:4 Isaiah 53:3

He First Loved Me

1 John 4:10

1. Recall a time when you dealt with a hurt that couldn't be soothed in and or your efforts?

2. Did you see God in the difficulty and did you ask Him for help?

3. Where are you possibly not taking God at His Word and then applying that truth in your daily life?

4. What is one small way you can see God working toward something good through this difficulty?

5. God loves you. What can you do differently today in order to live as a loved woman of God?

Continuing

"Not only so, but we also glory in our sufferings because we know that suffering produces perseverance."

Romans 5:3 NIV, ESV, NKJV

Have you found yourself on a journey that requires more than you feel you have to give? Perhaps you know yourself as one who starts many things but finishes few. If either of these fit you, then we should probably meet to commiserate. I'm pretty sure that I have struggled with weight since I was in the womb. I think food was my first friend, or at least I hung out with it way too much.

About seventeen years ago, I met an amazing lady who'd opened a new gym in my town, and after lots of inner nudging, I decided to find out what was within the doors of her place. I walked in, and she was right there in front of me. She said, "How can I help you?" I said, "Can you help me lose weight and get rid of this old lady?" She said point-blank, "Yes, I can." Well, then, I was speechless. Her solid response caused me to sign up, and I asked her where do we begin. Over a period of two years, this gifted lady taught me that the hardest thing to change was my thinking, not my body. She was correct. I worked hard with her as she worked even harder on me. She pushed me when I didn't want to be pushed and basically wanted to tell her to go away! But she understood going the distance for our personal best was a worthy goal. I lost over sixty pounds and had never been so strong; I felt really good about my body but even better about my mind. She taught me the power of overcoming myself.

As life continued moving forward, I successfully maintained that weight for five years. However, I found a weak spot in my commitment to myself in healthy eating and allowed poor choices to find their way back into my life. Now, she had not taught me this. She had taught me just the opposite. So, my choices were on me. Seventeen years later, I found myself back at my initial weight before I started with her. I was still very much involved with this lady, but my priorities changed for many reasons, not just one. I had chosen a little less self-discipline and a little more freedom but never considered the consequences of my choices, with which I was already familiar.

This past November, I got seriously tired of where I was. I had to come to terms with the unrest in my soul over settling for less when I had had the best. I'd worked hard for that outcome, and it was spectacular. My husband and I agreed that we would go on a keto diet together. I got books, read, and researched the way of eating, and he agreed we should try this. I also have a friend who wrote a best-selling book on intermittent fasting and decided I could add this, too. Let's just say losing breakfast was hard for this girl. I began to learn how to cook differently, and it was an adjustment. But I adjusted, settling for less without much loss. Sacrifice always has felt like loss, but extravagance is euphoric. Either way, they have significant outcomes.

So, why am I talking about "continuing" if I have found a method to follow that has good potential if I follow it? It has been seven months, and I've lost thirty pounds. I've been reminded that this is not a sprint; it's a long-distance race. I personally want this to go faster at times, and I'd really like some ice cream, thank you very much. I mean, it is summertime.

What I'm wrestling against is that my husband and I together determined that we were not setting a goal of a number of pounds lost but rather looking for a lifestyle. In choosing this path, we are required to "continue." There are lots of days that we would both probably tell you that we'd like to get off this ride of discipline and have a pizza for dinner and ice cream for dessert if we are honest, but the lifestyle is worth the discipline even on the hardest days. I'm so grateful to God that we are in this together because we all need others to come alongside us in the journey. God never intended for us to do this life in isolation. We need the connected support of others. We also need to be present in other people's lives to encourage them, even in the ugly things that we all must journey through. God promised us that suffering was something we would be familiar with. Jesus showed us the picture of suffering in laying HIS life down for us and then gave all of Himself up on the cross, ultimately, in love for us. I don't know anyone who could ever love any of us that much except, for Him.

So, on the days when I have been to the grocery store for my family for the week, and I have to handle lots of food, see the options I don't need, and watch others load up their buggies with things I could drool over (especially since its 10:00 a.m. and I hadn't eaten since 7:00 p.m. the night before and did I mention missing breakfast?), let's just say this isn't my most shining hour of the week! However, I am learning to overcome the power of my thinking rather than letting it overcome me. I am about winning the battle by "continuing."

God tells us to live one day at a time and to leave the troubles of tomorrow to tomorrow. Don't borrow those today. He keeps showing me that He is available in the "every day" of this. Above all, I see that He is teaching us to continue in this way so that we desire the change more than the old ways of thinking. Together, we have lost sixty-two pounds, and that's no small thing. We celebrate every pound leaving our bodies and rejoice over the fact that our bodies no longer have to carry that weight. Truly a burden lifted. We also realize that there will be days when we feel the sacrifice and the suffering and, yes, want to drive through some fast-food place and supersize something. However, we are confident that we can make a better choice together and "continue" to reap the rewards of this discipline of mind and body.

If you are in a place where you feel ready to throw in the towel of good choices and discipline, I encourage you to remember that there is no area of your life that God is not concerned with. He is here to give you what you need to continue. Tell Him what you feel, then tell yourself the truth: that this might be hard. Then remind yourself that Jesus understands exactly what it looks like to sacrifice the immediate for the best. He did it for you. You can do it too. Choose to continue with us.

Dear Father,

I'll be the first to raise my hand and admit that I am weak. I don't have what it takes to do this without You. Once again, You have provided me the view that I need to follow in a discipline that yields a better outcome for both my mind and my body. It's so easy to want what I want, Lord, but wanting what You want is what I desire most. God, help me to be as serious about these areas of life as I am about my soul. Keep me continuing in You, Lord.

And thank you for never letting me go farther than Your reach.

Amen.

2 Timothy 1:7 Hebrews 12:11 Isaiah 42:19

Continuing
Romans 5:3

1. What is something you work at continuing in your life?

2. Do you have a friend whom you share your struggles with and stay connected to?

3. When you struggle with commitments you have made with yourself, do you stop and look back honestly at what happened due to the struggle?

4. Can you pinpoint the trap that takes you down?

5. Bring your weakness to God by writing out a prayer to Him. Ask Him to help you overcome, one day at a time.

The One Still Standing

"He was man despised and rejected by men, a man of sorrows and acquainted with grief."

Isaiah 53:3

Have you known any mean girls in your days? Have you had that one who you were sure was out gunning for you from day one? Is there anything worse than rejection? Well, I am sure there are many other forms of rejection, but as a woman, it's never an easy pill to swallow. Sometimes, we know why it has occurred; other times, we are left with a void. That void can be much like that elephant in the room that no one talks about and yet all are aware of. When someone walks away, there is always one left standing. I'm not addressing being the one who walked away in these thoughts, but I have to give weight to both sides.

I wish I weren't as familiar with rejection as I am. If I look back on life to this point, I can see that I have been rejected on too many levels. If you think that I am the common denominator, then you would be accurate. But before you point a finger, please know that my purpose is to share with you how God met me, and He longs to meet you, too, if we trust Him with all of ourselves. Being rejected can trigger a spiral of downward thinking that, if not addressed, can send anyone into a dark hole that may not see any light for a very long time.

When we get wounded enough times, we either learn to stand, to fight, or to walk away. As I thought about this on a personal level, I tried to focus on Jesus and what He would do in these situations. For many years, there was hype over the statement, "What Would Jesus Do?" After the season of WWJD, the phrase just seemed to fade away. Yet the question remained: What Would Jesus Do in that situation you are in? What did He do when faced with those who rejected Him, opposed Him, plotted to kill Him, and simply walked away from a relationship with Him? In order to know Him and what He would do, we have to go back and take a long, hard look at Him in scripture and consider what we do know.

Jesus was compassionate, kind, generous, long-suffering, patient, loving, faithful, and so much more. But He was never passive. He stood on the truth of who He was through His words and actions. He was consistent and clear. The bottom line is that He faced more rejection than you and I could ever face. What does this mean for me, for us? It means that we are not alone in our rejection. In fact, we have one who has gone ahead of us and shown us how to continue through life's rejections.

Think about Jesus and Peter. They were very close and had traveled many roads together. When Peter saw Jesus calm the storm on the lake, his response to Jesus was to ask HIM to walk over to him. He succeeded in getting onto the water and yet began to sink when he thought about what he was doing. He took his sight off "who" was accomplishing this walk. Peter was that eager beaver who started well but didn't necessarily finish well. But he loved and believed in Jesus. He was verbal about his love for Jesus and eager to give testimony to Him. And yet, in the last days of Jesus's life, Peter denied that he knew Him. Not once, but three times he denied Christ.

I have known similar moments when the one walking closest to me through some hardship was suddenly gone from the place they'd filled alongside of me. It happened in a work setting for me. Now, granted, this person's relationship to me was not as developed as Christ and Peter's, but it was an invested relationship. In a matter of a few dark moments, the other individual denied anything and everything that had been held true between us. Call me crazy, but I was taken aback; no, I was floored. It was as if nothing that was true had ever occurred. In time, through examination and prayer over the outcomes, God helped me to see the root of the things that took place. I got it, and yet there was a personal level of rejection for me to continue to deal with because I really cared for this person, and her rejection was crystal clear. I didn't know how to get past it.

It was then that God began to show me, in our time alone together, that though I could not change what had occurred, I was not alone. He began to show me that Jesus knew exactly what I felt and where my thinking was. In fact, He'd survived such things in order to identify with me and my sufferings. He understood my every thought. He was there when this happened, and He knew how to overcome the outcome and give me the focus to continue. Like Peter, I had to take my eyes and place them fully on the one who calms the waves. I took that understanding and leaned hard into Him. When I struggled, I just said, Jesus, I know You are with me, and You've got this. Help me understand what I need to glean from this and move me forward to You. I did this often because it took my focus back to my original purpose, which was to serve Him through the work of my hands and give that work back to Him as my offering.

Yes, the elephant was still in the room when I 'd see anyone connected to that past event because there was unfinished work between us. But I have moved forward in purpose and continued instead to serve Christ beyond the rejection. It has no power over me. Christ lovingly put my eyes back on Him, and I found the ability to walk despite the waves of life.

Somewhere within myself, I know that I am stronger and more equipped to face the next rejection. But most of all, I know that Jesus fully knows what I feel, and He died for these sinful things out of love for me. He understands my heart, and I can identify with Him through the pains of rejection. No one can do that better than He. Isn't it great to have a "familiar" God? It keeps me in the position of thankfulness. I hope you find rest in that identification with the only One who truly knows our hearts.

Dear Father,

This is a tough one, yet You understand it personally. It's easy for me to think that it would have been nice if I just didn't have to face such a difficult task. But You went there before me, and You did it in love. You walked the path of rejection many times, and You know it well. You also know me well because You made me. Help me to lean into You as I learn to walk through rejection and not around it. Thank You for going ahead of me and for leaving me pictures of the rejection that You faced while You were here on Earth. You get it. Thank You for choosing me to follow You and for coming alongside of me in all things. Make me more and more like You.

Amen.

2 Corinthians 1:7 1 Peter 4:3 2 Corinthians 1:5

The One Still Standing
Isaiah 53:3

1. When you think of rejection, what comes to your mind? How do you identify with Jesus's sufferings?

2. What are some words you would use to describe Jesus's character?

3. Are you at all like Peter? If so, how?

4. What would you say is your typical response when you are rejected or wounded by another? Is your response seasoned with the character of Christ?

5. How will you choose to become more like Jesus when you rest on the truth? Explain.

Waiting on the Lord

"But they who wait for the Lord shall renew their strength; they shall mount up with wings like eagles; they shall run and not be weary; they shall walk and not faint."

Isaiah 40:31

If there is one test I will always fail it is the testing of my patience. I think I was born "ready." I don't mean like one of those people who can jump out of bed and shine automatically. Oh, no. That's definitely not me. But I am one who, once they are up and running, can keep going with fervor beyond her limits. I always pay later, but I can get it done. The problem is never in jumping on something for me. It is in waiting when I have a million ideas of accomplishing something and God says, wait. It just sends me into a struggle with myself. I'm quite sure that this is exactly the reason God says wait. He has a lot of work yet to do in me to accomplish this.

I find it always humbling when He lovingly tells me not to move on something but rather to wait on Him. I want to cry out, God, please, anything but waiting. Over the past three decades, I have had four back surgeries. In those seasons of great suffering and recovery, God got in my face and made it very clear to me that He loved me, and if all I did that day was sit in the chair and pray for others, I would have done the greatest thing of all. It was sobering and lifechanging. I knew that I could end up having the same problems with my back again and that brought great discouragement. I was halted from my going and my doing. I felt like a bird that had been put in a cage. I struggled with myself daily.

However, I began to take God at His Word, and I started praying specifically and intentionally. I prayed for anyone and everyone who came to my mind. I took each item and individual before the Lord and asked Him to bless them to meet their need. I never ran out of things to pray about. And then I began to see God work in those people's lives. Was it through my prayers? I could not meet their need, nor my own, but I knew the One who could.

I learned (in difficult ways) that prayer is crucial to our daily lives in all times that we face. It opens a daily dialogue with God that never ends. I can take my thoughts captive and bring each and every one to Him. In fact, He calls us all to this. The battles we face are primarily fought in our minds; Satan loves to stay between our ears and conflict our thoughts. It's in that thinking that we tend to lose course and seek our own answers to God's plan. However, the answer may be to wait on God. The most reassuring part of the above verse to me is that there is a point of overcoming that only arrives through our waiting. So, what are you tired of waiting on God for? Do you have a timeline of when God needs to answer your request? Trust me, He made the timeline, and His timing will be perfect. I can only say this to you in love because I have prayed over some things for over forty years, and during that time, God's call to me was to keep praying.

Sometimes, that meant tears, grief, restless nights, and endless longing. But the call was to "wait." I've wrestled hard against that position before Him. And yet, I have seen Him answer with great favor despite the wait. You see, He is training you and me today to learn to follow Him even in our waiting. Oh, my friend, it is hard, I know. My encouragement is to wrestle and yield. Then wait on God's best because He is faithful and hears every word you pray to Him. Keep asking; maybe together, we will become the best "waiters" ever.

Dear Father,

It sure is hard when You call on my greatest weakness for further strengthening. Help me to see that this is Your choice for me and for my strengthening and that, in time, I can continue to become more like You. Thank You, God, for loving me enough to make me uncomfortable to the point of conformity to Your will. Lord, in Your own timing please make me a great waiter. Take me into deeper prayer as I seek Your very heart.

Amen.

Psalm 37:34 Luke 6:12 1 Thessalonians 5:24

Waiting on the Lord

Isaiah 40:31

1. Do you struggle with waiting? Give an example.

2. When you struggle, how do you find your way to God for His help?

3. What is something that you are growing weary of as you wait for God to answer?

4. What can you do to help yourself continue in prayer over lengthy periods of waiting?

5. How is God changing your life through continued prayer?

Strength and Surrender

"I can do all things through him. Who gives me strength."

Philippians 4:13 NIV, ESV, NKJV

Do you find that you can feel utterly defeated before you even put your feet on the floor some mornings? Most women could probably say a strong *AMEN*. We ladies tend to keep our minds full of thoughts, and though we lie down at night and perhaps give those thoughts over to God, they seem to return with our first alertness. God tells us not to worry nor borrow the worries of tomorrow, because tomorrow will have enough worries of its own. If you're like me, the opportunities to worry are never few, and Satan loves to whisper them into my ear. Those "worry" temptations tend to drain me when I entertain them, and I lose the fight to overcome them. They also weaken my hope and faith in God. In those moments, I have to remind myself of the promises I have in God's Word.

These days, the world is discouraging, and the news only generates the prospect of greater worries and fear. Trying to shut all of it out is impossible, yet we must try to find the way through these obstacles with strength and surrender. The strength that only comes from God and surrenders to the things we think we have control over but truly do not. Never before have I known so fully that I must begin my days with the Lord and make extra sure He's the last one I talk to before I sleep. I need Him to get me beyond those "thoughts in my head." It's very easy to feel overwhelmed if we put our eyes on our own strength and forget to pursue the love and strength from the Father. I don't know about you, but I am fully confident that apart from God and HIS word, I will never accomplish it. Worries only weaken our hearts and limit our capacity to be effective tools in God's hands.

I see a twofold need in all of this. We are constantly in need of strength and perpetually tempted to become weak. For me, this puts things in clearer perspective. I already know I don't have adequate strength to overcome the challenges of a day before it begins. I have to choose to get strengthened before I charge out of the door or just hobble to the coffee maker.

The biggest step I believe we must take each day is to take up our cross and follow Christ. In order to do that we have to make sure that we are not in the way of seeing His plan. To do that, we have to go first to Him and tell Him that we need Him, admitting that we don't have what it takes. Then we must seek His will, ask Him what we need, and for that which is ahead of us and unseen.

We know how to pray for the things ahead of us that we know are coming. But how do we pray for the things unseen? We pray with faith and expectation that the Spirit will go before us and with us. Prayer is the vehicle that God has given us to meet every obstacle. Chaos tends to show up most days, but the reminder we have to hang on to is that God is in control. We have to tell ourselves the truth over and over again. The truth will equip us to endure for the cause of Christ for that day. We can remind ourselves, when we don't seem able to pray, that Jesus Himself is praying for us. What encouragement!

The battles of the day will always be with us, but we must take up the "sword of the Spirit" each day, the Bible, so that we are able to fight off temptations. Expect the battle, and in the meantime, study God's Word and hide it in your heart by memory. Surround yourself with it; when you need it most, you will have it deep in your heart.

I don't know where I'd be if I couldn't read God's Word every day. I don't want to know. He has taught me that my full reliance on Him begins in the Bible with the dawn of each new day. You and I don't have what it takes to do the days or the nights, but God loved us and sent His son. That son, Jesus, made a way for us to come to Him at every moment and find what we need. That's the truth that will get us through any day. Make God your first priority today. Seek Him, and you will indeed find Him. Call on Him while you can. He is ever faithful, and through Christ, you truly will be able to do "all things."

Dear Father,

We acknowledge that apart from You, we are unable to handle, even face, the battles ahead in this day. Father, would You help me to make You the priority of this day? Would You speak to me through Your holy Word and bring Your Holy Spirit alongside of me as I seek to follow and serve only You? Bring the light of Christ toward my heart this day and help me to love as Jesus loves. I will fail, Father, and You will still be there. Thank You, Father, for Your faithfulness.

Amen.

John 14:6 Isaiah 55:6 Hebrews 10:23

Strength and Surrender
Philippians 4:13

1. What tends to be a worry that you struggle with repeatedly?

2. Do you seek God for strength and help to surrender the worries that are not under your control?

3. How have you surrounded yourself with truth to help you through the temptation to worry?

4. How are you applying prayer to your worry or temptation to worry?

5. What are some ways you are learning to turn worries into hope for yourself and others?

Peace Within

"Peace I leave with you; my peace I give to you. Not as the world gives do I give to you. Let not your hearts be troubled, neither let them be afraid."

John 14:27

What are some things that create fear in you? I could start with snakes and add cars hitting me while I'm walking in a parking lot. Unfortunately, I have experienced both, and I have a genuine fear. I struggled in those circumstances to find peace that overcame my fear. I knew that God could give me peace because the Bible tells me this. But I wrestled with the fear and longed for peace. What are some of the daily life things that steal your peace?

Most women, I think, would list worry, insecurities, unrest in our marriages or families, and misplaced priorities that rob us of that God-given peace. The world repeatedly tells us that we should be able to handle life and its chaos. It tells us that we can find peace through a multitude of "things." It offers us all kinds of artificial peace. Not true peace though. The kind that only comes from God. When our hearts are lacking peace, no one has to tell us. We are the first ones to know. In a sense, it's like being hungry and realizing that you failed to eat anything for several hours. That hunger signals to your stomach and body that something is missing. What do we do? We grab something to eat, wait about twenty minutes, and bingo, we feel better.

So, how do we feed that need when we feel that lack of peace? I know that I need to get quiet and silence the world to figure out what has robbed my heart of that peace. I often ask God to show me the obstacle in or around me that encroaches on His gift of peace. That is often followed by a recognition of the source and some humble repentance on my part. My mind has learned that to race through life is the goal we are all to achieve. However, that couldn't be farther from God's instructions to us. The verse also tells us, "Let not your hearts be troubled nor afraid." When my mind travels the path of retracing, it is not long before I find my heart very troubled, indeed stressed out.

Don't you hear people talk about being stressed out often? If you are like me, you take on a thought you don't need to get stuck on and persevere. Satan has a party keeping that process going in your mind, and before you know it, you're not only troubled, but now you have some irrational fear about something totally unrelated.

Where does God's peace go in those moments? We tend to look at Him figuratively and ask something like, do you see this? Or think, I could really use a hand with this, God. And yet, God did not remove an ounce of our peace. We traded it for something less than God's best. In a time when the world seems to be in unrest continually, what more do we need than to know the inner peace that God offers us? So, how do we overcome this temptation to give away our God-given peace so very easily? You won't love this answer, and I can't say I did either, but it's true.

We have to practice the peace that passes all understanding. In order to do this, we have to study the peace that we have from God daily and identify the things that get in the way of experiencing it. It requires us to be honest with ourselves. I have found many times that I am the one guilty of forfeiting that peace. I have allowed things and circumstances that I did not need to take on by myself and removed them from the hand of God. Before I know it, I have taken myself out of the place of peace. I grab hold and take on something that was never intended to be in my hand.

I will say very honestly that this is an ongoing process for me. I must continue to fight against the things that call me to respond in my own ways, that only bring me into a state of trouble and cause me to become worn out. It means that I have to go to God before making decisions to hear what He thinks first. It means that at times, I have to say no, or I don't know, rather than get into peace-robbing situations. I have to advocate for my own heart on a daily basis proactively. This does not occur for me unless I get quiet with Him first.

It's important to understand here that the peace I'm speaking of is not that of a serene setting. I am rather referring to peace that is within, a rightness of spirit, a place of still certainty. A place without trouble, stress, or fear. It is a place where the confidence of Christ reigns within me and yields stability. I'm more certain of what peace "is" because of the unrest I have experienced over the years. I've known some great fear. I am thankful to say I survived having a semi-automatic pistol held in my face by a couple seeking to rob me one evening after dark in a busy store parking lot. The physical and mental response to the experience took a long time to overcome. I had to really work on the specific fears that I experienced after that. I had to release them over time and find God's peace that remained. I found the desire to overcome, and everything in me needed peace in the place of trouble.

In all things, God has a purpose, and now, years later, I can see how He chose to use this to make me more aware of the world around me, to understand that evil is real and that He is always out ahead of me. I am constantly in need of His greater view of all things. I've used this true story to warn other women not to do at night what they can do in the daylight, especially around the holidays. I've used what God took me through to teach others how to be wise and protect that God-given peace that is theirs.

There will always be "peace robbers" out there waiting for us to buy in, and yet we have to determine just how valuable that peace is to us and then not settle for anything less than its presence in our souls. Take the time today to do some soul-searching and ask yourself the hard questions. Am I giving my peace away? Take the time to get quiet with God before you get going. That peace is worth so much. Make sure that, like with a clogged drain, you do the hard work to get the junk out and get that peace flowing as intended. Love God.

Dear Father,

Thank You for seeing my need for peace, Your peace. The world offers me lots of things that will look like peace, but Lord, I know they never satisfy my soul like the peace I've known from You. There is no match for it. Teach me, Father, to abide in Your peace and, in doing so, eliminate the troubled and fearful places that eat at my soul by my own invitation. I trust in You.

Amen.

Romans 15:33 Philippians 4:7 Romans 15:13

Peace Within
John 14:27

1. What are some things that you find cause you to be fearful?

2. Which of the fears listed in paragraph two do you struggle with?

3. Do you see a trigger or pattern in your losing sight of peace within? What can you do to interrupt that process?

4. What things can you eliminate or put into your day to help you when you need a greater sense of peace?

5. What helps you practice the peace of God that has been given to you in Christ? Are there places and practices that help you to increase your awareness of God's peace?

Heart of a Servant

"Have this mind among yourselves, which is yours in Christ Jesus, who, though he was in the form of God, did not count equality with God something to be grasped, but emptied himself, by taking the form of a servant, being born in the likeness of men."

Philippians 2:5-7

What do you think of when I say the word servant? Do you immediately think of dining out and the waitstaff? Or do you think about nobility and those of the upper class who have others who take care of their daily needs and wants? Probably my least favorite job ever is that of a full-time servant. They have long days and nights. They are constantly in a position to respond and, at times, without any warning.

When I was in college, I worked for a season at a well-known fast-food restaurant. I was living and going to school in a town that could easily be referred to as a "college town." There were residents in the town, but mostly, there were tons of college students. One thing that I learned during that time was that college students are hungry at all hours of the day and night. One day, after cooking French fries for eleven hours, I was exhausted. That particular evening, in the last hour of being open, a bus came through with a college sports team. They were ordering food like this was the first meal they'd had in weeks.

I took a big breath and realized that this was a good time to see how good I was at completing the challenge and not losing my mind. I wasn't very focused on serving. My thoughts were, how can I get this done, close the front doors, clean the stations, and not slide across the floor before I finish? I mean, who needs an ice skating rink? Just show up in a fast-food restaurant where they fry anything at closing, and you won't need skates. You'll just need a great deal of balance. We got the orders all taken care of, and the door locked, but after hours. I did not, however, leave that night feeling much like a servant. I had more of the attitude of a slave.

I think back over that time now and realize that I had to practice a lot of patience in that job. I loved meeting people, taking care of their requests, and sending them on their way with a smile. But that was not all that I was responsible for in my duties as a servant. I had the less attractive parts of serving, too. During those times of cleaning the toilet, I had lots of opportunity to consider what my heart of service really looked like.

Jesus was a generous servant while living on the earth. We have so many pictures in the Bible of Jesus's life and how, as a servant, He met the needs of others. I think particularly about the little boy with the five loaves of bread and the five fish. Jesus looked at what He did have before He made it into enough. In the end, Jesus not only met all of the people's needs, but they had excess. I had to ask myself, do I look at what I do have or immediately focus on what I don't have? What was I missing of Jesus in my moment of service? I found I had shifted my focus from whom I was serving to what I was serving.

Back then, I was a hungry Christian. I had encircled myself with people who would steer me toward a deeper walk with God. So, I definitely struggled with this situation. I wanted to know more about how to be like Christ, yet I realized there was still so much of me in the picture. I at times felt defeated in my faith and following. But God saw my immaturity and answered my prayers, one shift at a time. It was in the enduring that I learned what service really looked like. It became crystal clear that my heart was not in the right place. I came to understand that the service I brought came from one of two places and that the choice was up to me. It wasn't complicated. If my heart was in the wrong place, then my actions would follow.

It took great humility for Christ to take up this role of servant, which we see in Philippians 2. Though He had every right to every aspect of what it meant to be God, He chose the position of a servant. This, my sisters, is humility of a right heart. Perhaps, like me, you've lost your direction at times. If this is your struggle, too, know that it can be changed.

Those years in college were great growing years for me. God used the time to get my full attention and passion for Him. He also generously taught me how He wanted to change my heart to be more like His. I wanted this to happen. It cost me a great deal. But hopefully, I have come to understand something I've lived by since that time. My purpose then as now is to treat other people as I want to be treated. I knew that I had to live with a serving heart in order to be like Jesus. It helped me greatly to keep my thinking on others and the work of esteeming them as more important than myself. In doing so, my desire to serve only grew greater.

Like many things we learn along the journey with Christ, this was not a lesson to grasp and then check off the list. It has been an ongoing lesson. The flesh loves to jump up and say, hey, what about me? When this happens in me, I know for certain that I need a self-check in humility and heart. Because Jesus laid down His life for me, I, too, can lay down my life for others. So, is it time for your heart to get a checkup? How long has it been since your last appointment? If you find that you can't recall the last time you went there, then it is time. Go to God and tell Him that you need a heart adjustment, and lay down the things that need to go before Him. He'll meet you there.

Dear God,

Thank You for the mundane things in life that You bring to the forefront of our thinking to teach us to be like You. Father, I'll be the first to admit that is hard to do. I'd like to blame the world and all of the selfishness around me, but it doesn't take away the condition of my own heart. Father, make me like David and grow in me a heart that wants all of You. I've failed so many times, yet You continue lovingly teaching me of Your generous forgiveness and love even for me. Help me to take that love in service to others around me today, Lord. It is my prayer.

Amen.

Philippians 2:3 John 15:13 Matthew 23:11

Heart of a Servant
Philippians 2:5-7

1. What are some ways that you serve on a regular basis?

2. What is your least favorite area of serving and why?

3. What have you learned about having a heart of service that reflects Christ?

4. Do you wrestle against God's will for you to serve? How can you overcome that?

5. Where is God asking you to lay down your desires with humility and serve as Christ did?

Light in the Darkness

"For you save a humble people, but the haughty eyes you bring down. For it is you who light my lamp; the LORD my God lightens my darkness."

Psalm 18:27-28

Dark moments of life often linger long after they have taken place. They tend to come up and remind us of the light that is ours through Christ despite the dark moments. I don't want to know what the darkness is like without having His all-consuming light. Is God the light in your lamp, or are you depending on other things to brighten your days? Life brings us challenges that none of us can foresee. It weaves a path of unexpected twists and turns. Sometimes, those challenges yield great outcomes over time. However, many leave us short of breath, anxious, and feeling lost.

One of those times for me was at the last hours of my father's life. He had lived a long and full life. I was fully aware that he would not always be here with us, but when he left, I had the reality in hand that he was indeed gone. There was a profound darkness in those moments. I knew that God was very much with me, but I felt the sting of death as it came to him. I'd seen suffering, and its imprint was burned into my heart. I knew that this was a time to remind myself of the truths I had hidden in my heart over the years. God was with me; He knew what He was doing, and He would keep me in perfect peace if my mind stayed on Him.

My dad's passing came during the Covid years, and though he did not die from the virus, life was very different. As a society, we were learning to live in isolation and detachment. Being around others was just not the acceptable thing to do. After his passing I considered the darkness in my soul. I found great help and light in reflecting on our visits of the previous two years. Our relationship was not an easy place to be at times. And yet, in those last years, together, we found some light and common ground in Christ. You see, God took my dad home to isolation to protect his health, but through his computer, he found a whole world of Christian pastors who spoke to his aging heart. He would tell me about his Sundays in those days. He would listen to five different sermons, and then in the afternoon, he'd do a Sunday School lesson with a friend on the phone.

He and I began discussing some deeper issues about God and the light He sheds on our paths. Dad was seeing things for the first time in many ways. Now, those warm memories with him keep me smiling despite the darkness of death that would, in time, turn to full light for him. You see, my dad didn't get everything right, just as I won't. And yet, He was learning, even to the end, that

God was indeed the light shining through his very own darkness all along the way. Seeing that revealed to him was a gift to me. He was becoming humbled in an all-new way. It was as if he finally got it.

He had lived thinking that he understood who God was and what was in His Word. However, he came to the realization that he knew only in part. Yes, he had lots of knowledge about God, but he lacked a personal, humbled relationship that was fully dependent on God. He did his best to live in the light of Christ, but things were still not clear to him. He was aware of this and wrestled a long time with this thought. I recall the day he phoned me and said my name loudly. He was excited about what he had discovered in the Bible and wanted to see if I knew it, too. I assured him that I clearly understood the things that he was bringing to me.

Having been a mother and now a grandmother, I have seen great joy and wonder in the eyes of little ones as they discover the things of life. So many things are new; there are lots of firsts. The element of surprise always seems to be fresh and new. But this was the expression of my ninety-one-year-old father. At that point, I knew that God was lighting his lamp even as life dimmed.

God has been good to show us in our own personal challenges that His illumination is not only still available, but it is shining brightly even when we can't see it. He is the light in our darkness, and we can rest in that truth. As we reach to God and rely on His mercy and grace, He will meet us. He will see to our vision clearing from the dark and transition us into the full glory of His eternal light. Are you facing some dark place that you feel certain will never lift? Have you wandered from the light of Christ and felt that absence? Be certain that He feels your pain and absence; He feels it all. His desire is to love you through this challenge, even when you don't feel it, and see you safely to the other side of it. He is a good God who holds you in His mighty hand. Reach for Him today and let that light shine in you anew and afresh. He is able and ready to fill you.

Dear Father,

In the Psalms, David tells us that there is nowhere that we can run or hide from You. Thank You, Lord, for Your watchful eye over us, always. Teach us true humility as we journey with You, Lord. In the dark times, would You please remind us that You are the light of the world and that in You, we can find our way? Thank You for Your light that will never grow dim.

Amen.

Ephesians 26:3 Psalm 112:4 Psalm73:23

Light in the Darkness
Psalm 18:27-28

1. Where is a place in your life that feels dark and needs God's light?

2. How does God's presence in your daily life help you apply His light in your dark moments? Give an example.

3. Do you struggle in lingering darkness for a past time that you desire to bring fully into the light?

4. What will you look to God for clarity on today? What is He revealing to you?

5. Do you find hope in the light of Christ no matter what the darkness feels like? Give an example of that hope from a past struggle.

Love with Purpose

"Love bears all things,
hopes all things,
endures all things."

1 Corinthians 13:7

I have a wonderful, crazy husband who could not be any more the opposite of me if he tried. I don't think I've ever known anyone whose preferences are so far from my own. Today, for kicks, I asked him what color I should get on my toenails, and he said, whatever color makes you happy! That was the answer of a seasoned husband, a safe answer. Then I told him, I'll get camouflage, you love camouflage. He didn't even laugh. But I laughed enough for us both.

Marriage is the first picture of love that we see in the Garden of Eden. God had created man "in His own image." Then He knew man would need a "suitable helper," and He made woman. I've perhaps said this too many times, but Adam and Eve were surrounded with good things and each other in their nakedness. I'm sure they figured out what to do with their time. They knew no shame or sin before they ate the forbidden fruit.

But marriage isn't a bed of roses for most of us. Instead, it is hard work with many beautiful moments interwoven. I was thinking about the fact that my sweet husband was made in God's image. Then I asked myself the hard question. Do I see God in him when I look at him? My response is that I definitely see God in him, but I wondered if

I saw him as created in God's image. All of a sudden, I was thinking differently about him. I know that I, too, am made in the image of God, but the image of my husband took on a new dimension.

Society would find problems with my words to you, but if God made my man in His image, then how was I to see him? Sometimes, I honestly don't feel very loving toward my husband. For example, when I couldn't find the thing that I put in a particular place a week ago because he has found it a new place. I feel lots of things when he says, oh yeah, it's right here (like I had a clue). At that point, I had to remind myself that "love bears all things." It's never the first thought that pops into my head, so don't put that on yourself, either. Several things might pop into my head at that moment, and a few of them may pop right out of my mouth. Then, I find myself needing to apologize for them later on. But if I am seeing him more like God made him, can my thinking shift from seeing him in his maleness, to his God likeness?

Perhaps you are like us, and you've had some stressful seasons in your marriage. Times when nothing seems to be furthering your relationship, and it feels as if it is unraveling at the seams. I'm reminded of one time in particular that we went through. We struggled for about two months. We were communicating poorly, if at all. Our silence did not help either one of us. But in time, we sought some godly counsel and found the short road back to our path with each other, and we were back on solid footing. During that long stretch of time that we struggled, I was determined to be hopeful. I had to choose to believe that things could change. I remember praying hard and often for God to move the obstacles that stood in our way. And He did.

I had to choose to look beyond what I could see and trust God for what I could not see, only hope for. God did indeed bring us through the struggles and made us better for the experience. Our choices and dependence on God in both the good times and the bad determine if our love grows or dies.

Has your husband ever done something that you thought was unforgivable? There are some offenses that are not acceptable biblically, but all are potentially forgivable. Again, the disclaimer may be hard. But love grows through the seasons of our lives. It is not stagnant. It differs through the days and becomes stronger through the hard places. My parents were a picture of this to me in many ways. They had an unusual marriage; let me be careful here. About a year after my mother had passed away, I was with my dad for a visit. I asked, Dad, what do you miss most about mom? Now, my dad wasn't an emotional creature, but I was looking for some expression of depth or feeling. You know, some heartfelt-love kind of thing. Nope, being in true character, he said, I miss fighting with her. That was something they had really mastered in sixty-four years of marriage. He was being serious. It was not exactly what I was looking for, but somehow, I really understood his statement. They could spar and weren't often kind to one another, but they loved each other. There was no question of that in my mind.

Love that goes the distance is seasoned through bearing up under tough circumstances, staying hopeful when there seems to be no reason to, and enduring the hard places in order to experience the even better ones. Love is a choice. God gave us lots of wisdom and understanding of love through His Word. He put the framework of "how to love" in I Corinthians 13 when He spelled out what it is and what it is not. He made it so much easier, or at least much clearer, to be understood.

So, how are you doing in terms of seeing your man as God's creation? For me, when I remind myself of Whom he belongs to and was made by, it is easier to put up with things that I don't want to. I am able to stay open-minded and be grateful for every day we are given. I see God in him and in the creation he is. I view him more as a beautiful piece of artwork rather than a problem I have to deal with. It helps me to remind myself of how God loves me despite myself. Whatever the case, we have the choice to love with purpose. If we are in Christ, then we have His love in us and in His example through God's Word, the Bible. We've not been left to wonder. Take those truths today and love in new and strengthened hope.

Dear God,

Thank You for creating us all in Your image and likeness. Thank You for the words in scripture that we can reach for and learn from if we allow You to take them into our hearts and minds. Teach us, Lord, and give us a willing spirit, especially in the tough times. Lift our eyes up to see the hope that is ours in You, both of us. Protect what You have given us, Lord, and keep us on the path that leads to love and life in You.

Amen.

John 13:34 John 15:12 1 John 4:11

Love with Purpose

1 Corinthians 13:7

1. Do you see your husband as he is, created in the image of God?

2. What qualities in your husband reflect God's image to you?

3. What change are you hoping for in your marriage that you don't see yet?

4. How can you help yourself continue when nothing in you feels loving toward your spouse?

5. What does it mean to love with purpose? Write out your answer.

Community through Connection

"A new commandment I give to you, that you love one another: just as I have loved you, you are also to love one another."

John 13:34

Communication today is a digital highway that consists of messaging, texting, and emailing. I recently had someone text me to ask if they could call me and talk. I sat confused over that for a bit, and then I called her. I told her, you don't have to text me to see if you can call, just try me. She said that's not how it's done these days. You text before calling. I found that to be the oddest thing I had heard in a long time. I felt like the concept sounded like a person had to get permission to call then. I'm sorry, but that makes absolutely no sense to me and what I understand of communication.

There's an old song entitled "The Times They Are A-Changin'." I remember it well, but I don't think it even gets close to where we are in today's versions of change. I couldn't let this concept go, and I chewed on this idea of asking permission to talk, or at least this was my interpretation of it. My mind drifted to the scriptures that might give me clarity on this concept. After much thought, I came to the conclusion that if this was the way to address communication, then there probably weren't a lot of person-to-person conversations going on.

I will admit that I love being able to text someone, and it is a bit easier than talking to a person about some topics or issues. However, I know that text and emails, along with other social media options, leave a certain amount of room for wrong interpretation and misperceived tones. These things don't get lost in an actual conversation.

My further thinking took me to what this looks like for the body of Christ and, more specifically, for women who thrive on relationships with other women. I asked myself, am I spending my time in more relationships that don't involve actually talking to another person, or am I engaging in active conversations? Am I reaching the women around me who are influenced by words as well as experiences in communication? The question was a personal challenge for me. I had to admit some things to myself and see things as they really are. I have made it a practice to spend time with people as a result and have face-to-face relationships. And yes, I like a good long conversation with my best girls occasionally. We laugh and struggle, share our likes and dislikes, and offer support to one another through the assurance and reminder that we are not alone. We have one another. I can't say a text would cover what that conversation would, ever.

I came to a somewhat sobering realization that in order to be in community with other women we have to connect. When we are together, we can have a first-person experience and can see, hear, and interact with the other person in the moment. There is a familiarity that develops between us and the other person just by being in each other's presence. Communicating only through text or messaging often limits our interpretation of the message and can perhaps lead to thinking that was never intended. Many of us have probably played the gossip game before, where you whisper a message into the next person's ear. They, in turn, whisper the message to the next person, and so on. In the end, what often comes from the final person has nothing to do with the original message. I happen to think that this is an accurate example of what can happen through a text or message when the interpretation is just based on words. So much of communication is enhanced with expression, intonation, or inflection of voice that exceeds the words they accompany.

We are accustomed to investing time in our spouses and family, but relationships between believers also require time and priority. I cannot say what scripture would look like if Jesus had owned a cell phone and had technology at His fingertips. Those things would still be secondary to what He gave us in His own example in the four gospels of the New Testament.

Jesus gave us the command to love one another, and He set the example before us in the Bible. He demonstrated lots of community through actual connection with the people who lived alongside of Him. He was always "with" the people, His disciples, His Father. He connected with the people He was with. He had real relationships that revealed the actual hearts of those He was with. I think of Zacchaeus or the woman at the well. Jesus was bold with Zacchaeus and told him to come down out of the tree because he was going to have dinner with him at his house. And the woman at the well? If that conversation had not taken place and she had not had her life reflected back to her through Jesus's words, she'd have never become a believer that day.

We have many examples of what loving one another looks like from God in His Word. The question is, are we going to change God's way of doing things in an effort to find a more current way of doing things? I will not be making that change. I need the community that only comes through connection, and I believe you do, too. In order to continue in Christ, I know that I have to take the more challenging path at times and bypass that text in order to turn it into a real conversation with myself and another. I think that somewhere along the lines, people decided that texting someone is faster than having a conversation. I would ask if in doing this that you've found yourself in fewer relationships of significance?

We were created for relationship, and God planned it in just this way. He never intended for us to separate and isolate. His intention is for us to pursue one another and engage in life together so that we might know one another and His plans for us. We need community more than ever before and much is driving us in the opposite direction. Are you letting yourself drift into that place of compromise? Do you feel lonely or isolated? Can you just be quiet and have peace within? Or are you unsettled? Maybe it's time to reach out to a real person with a real conversation and some face-to-face time. Let me be the first to encourage you to go there. Reach out and see what God has for you on the other side of that conversation. You might just find a new peace within.

Dear Father,

I'm so grateful for the example that You've given me in my relationship with You. I'm living for the day when we can have a face-to-face conversation. Help me to see that for this part of my journey with You that I am to look for You in others who love and serve You too. Keep me on the path that follows the example You set for me in Jesus while He was here on earth. Finally, Father, thank You for other people and the privilege I have in community and connection with them. I see Your purpose in it all.

Amen.

1 Corinthians 12:12 John 17:21 John 10:15

Community through Connection
John 13:34

1. What does the balance look like for you between live conversations and nonverbal conversations? Which is greater, less?

2. What do you enjoy about having live conversations with other women?

3. Whom did you last spend time with in a face-to-face and what did you take away from the time? List a few things.

4. What example has Jesus set for you to follow in relationships of love with others?

5. Are you connected to a community of believers? If not, is this something that God wants you to address? How?

God's Best Yes

"But as for me, I will look to the Lord;
I will wait for the God of my salvation;
my God will hear me."

Micah 7:7

Have you been in a situation where you were unsure what response is the correct one to give? I'm thinking the more appropriate question is probably, how many times a day do you find yourself unsure whether an answer should be yes, no, or wait? I could probably set records if I were counting my own and you might feel the same way. There are many things in life that we struggle with, but for me I'd have to rank that concept "wait" at the top of my list. If I am honest with you, I have always struggled with patience. I am a "get it done" kind of girl who does not want to have to go back and fix something after the fact. I want it to be right the first time. However, I have come to understand that the majority of my life has been lessons in waiting. Thank goodness I like to learn things or I'd have probably lost my mind by now.

It's been a hard lesson to this point and still is a struggle when God does not give me a clear answer in a short amount of time. One of the struggles I've had in learning this is that others often want us to respond to their question before God has answered us. At times that can look as if I am being negligent to the waiting individual. I like to be prompt and yet God always answers on His own timetable. I feel like I have to explain that to others or choose an answer before I have one, which usually turns out badly. That's when I often find out that I stopped short of God's best yes. It's taken a lot of my impatience and God's patient prodding to get me to the place where I can just voice when I feel that pressure is driving my decision, rather than God's answer.

Perhaps you struggle with this too. I am learning to wait for God's best. It seems like the older I get the bigger the decisions are and their ramifications greater. Somehow I thought this would get simpler; it has not. What I have found is that I am getting stronger in waiting on the Lord. The world might refer to that as weakness rather than strength, but God tells us repeatedly in scripture to wait for Him. That's when I raise my proverbial hand and ask, then why am I so impulsive and impatient? The answer is not that hard, really. God is taking that energy He's put in me and He is honing it into a usable resource for "good." By yielding to His best yes, I learn the difference between my first choices and His. It's not easy but I am starting to get it.

We may want God to give us a quick, clear answer when we pray to Him and seek which way we should go with something, but we don't have an answer until He gives it. I find myself at times apologizing to God for not waiting on Him. I do feel like a true child of God when I am waiting for an answer. It does not feel comfortable because it goes against my fallen flesh. It does not bring me peace at times, and yet I find a certain assurance that I am right in the middle of His holy will while I am waiting. I know that my heavenly Father is showing me, His child, the way in which He has for me to go. I can ultimately rest in that place.

I was once offered a great opportunity for a position. From all worldly and godly perspective, it was a great opportunity for me, for anyone. But as soon as I began to pray about it, I felt a hesitation. I continued to pray, and time was drawing near for a decision; did I mention I don't do indecisiveness well? I knew that I did not have a certainty about saying yes. I could fully see myself handling the role, and it was an honor even to be asked. And yet God was not saying yes. I had already been to my husband and asked him to pray with me for this decision. Still, nothing led to the answer being yes. Because I don't like to disappoint people I was not looking forward to giving my response, which was no.

I made the call and gave my response, at which point Satan jumped in to let me know just how guilty I should feel for that decision. But he never wins, and in time I got to see the absolutely perfect individual take the role and I got to rejoice with her. This decision was a very personal journey for me with God. I knew that I was seeing His direction through my persistent prayers.

The greatest lesson I learned through this, and so many of these times of question, is that God's timing and answer is the only answer. If it means waiting, then I wait and pray on. If there is no specific yes, then the answer for me is no, if the decision is time-sensitive. But, I do not move forward without His best yes. No, I don't always understand where things are going, but that is when I remind myself that God has not asked me to know what's ahead. He has only called me to do today and wait on Him for what tomorrow will bring.

One final thought: I find that when I go to sleep on a question and rise up ready to hear from Him the next morning, He answers. There is clarity in every new day that we are given and if He does not answer in that day, then pray on. He has the answer and you don't want less than His "best yes."

Dear Father,

Thank You for hearing my every asking of You. I know that when I ask You to show me the way, You will answer. I'm certain that I don't know what's best for me. Thank You for continuing to teach me how to wait for You patiently. Thank You for the courage to say no. It isn't hard when I know it is from You. Thank You for Your faithfulness to me. I want Your best yes.

Amen.

Psalm 69:13 Psalm 66:19 Matthew 21:22

God's Best Yes
Micah 7:7

1. Do you seek God's answers to choices you are making throughout your days?

2. Do you put pressure on yourself to make decisions when God has not given you the answer yet?

3. When you wait on God for decisions, how do the outcomes differ from what you would have chosen on your own?

4. What do you do in the meantime while waiting on God to answer?

5. Is waiting something God wants to grow in your life? How will you respond to this call from Him?

Lacking in Nothing

"Fear not, for I am with you; be not dismayed, for I am your God; I will strengthen you, I will help you, I will uphold you with my righteous right hand."

Isaiah 41:10

Do you ever find yourself feeling empty? You aren't sure what is missing, but you just feel an absence that you wish you could explain? The word empty means, "containing nothing, lacking meaning or having no value or purpose." As a woman and a Christian, I can say that I have at times felt lacking of meaning within. During those times of uncertain purpose, and the sense of being alone or empty, I am tempted to think that God has moved. I'm also very tempted to think that I have done something to prompt Him to distance from me. Nothing could be farther from the truth at that point. The truth is that I belong to God, He is always with me, and through His filling me with His Spirit, I am never lacking.

In the early years of my walk with Christ I experienced a great deal of emptiness. It took time for me to see where I had filled my own life and where God was now filling me. I had learned to rely on myself first, not God. I knew I fell short and had tons of insecurities to back that up. The emptiness, however, was not from God; He had come into my life and taken it for His own. The void I felt was often a reflection of my own ability to meet the things in my life that God was asking me to give over to Him. Surrender was not easy.

At times, that sense of lostness can be the result of pain within me. At other times I can feel a sense of dryness in my soul. All of these are symptoms that lead me back to one question. What has changed? I find this to be the right time to sort out my feelings and God's truth. The mixing of the two never yields truth. Sometimes the void I've felt has led me to seek a solution through digging deep into the promises that God has made to me. They are found in only one place, God's holy Word.

Several years ago, I began to memorize verses of scripture that contained His promises. I found many truths that I cling to and apply to every day of my life. Truths like, I am always with you, I go before you, I live to intercede for you. I talk to Him about my feelings and ask Him for more of His truth. He has promised that He will never leave me, nor forsake me, that He (alone) knows everything about me because He made me. I'd say I am never alone, nor are you. We have a great source to reach for within us when we are walking in God's truths and not our own resources.

There will be times when we all feel depleted, or perhaps defeated. Those are real times and yet even then God is right there with us. You may face a battle head-on and yet you do not face it alone.

Jesus did some hard things in His living years on Earth and we will too. That has been spelled out for us in the Bible. But the good news is that we will never be alone or empty of God when we belong to Him. So, I'd ask you in love, are you spending time with God and getting to know Him more intimately? Are you digging into His Word and searching for His promises to you?Let me encourage you to make time to do both. You'll know the reality of His presence anew in doing so.

Father God,

Thank You for loving me today and for calling me by my name as Your child. You know my tendency to look to myself before I look to You and I ask that You would change this in me daily. Help me to commit time to You and Your Word that I am grow closer and closer to You. Thank You for Your filling that compares to none other.

Amen.

Matthew 28:20 Psalm 73:23 Colossians 2:5

Lacking in Nothing
Isaiah 41:10

1. Is there anything that we can do to remove ourselves from the hand of God?

2. What causes you to forget that God is with you and that He has you?

3. When you sort out your feelings next to God's truth, what are the differences?

4. Can God handle your fear and help you overcome it? Have you identified it to Him?

5. What truths do you need to hear every day to help you find security in God's right hand, which is holding you?

Practicing the Presence of God

"Let me hear in the morning of your steadfast love, for in you I trust. Make me know the way I should go, for to you I lift up my soul."

Psalm 143:8

I'm not sure where you are as you dig into these words, but I do know that you are looking for more of God. One of the many challenges that God has put before me in this lifetime has been to ask myself if I am seeing Him in light of His constant presence with me. It's very easy for me to seek God's Word and even spend time with Him and then leave Him right there with my books and Bible. For a long time, I didn't see that the quiet time I was spending with Him was not just a stopping point in my day. Through God's love and work on my heart I began to see that the point of those quiet times was to focus myself on Him and then continue in Him as I moved forward. What a difference that made.

Seeing God as waiting to meet me each day and realizing that from there He would lead me, was a new concept. And yet the more I began to take His words in scripture as my own, the more I saw the continuum of what walking with God really looks like. I soon began to realize that this was what it meant to "practice the presence" of God. Rather than jumping into a new day and then grabbing for God when things started to go down the tube, I began by learning to continue with Him. I had to check myself often to be sure that I had not left

Him on the curb of my life again. This took a lot of effort on the part of my ADD brain.

I knew that the effort was mine to make if I was going to learn to practice living in God's presence moment by moment. I wanted it; I wanted more of Him. The choice was one worth making. I failed miserably and frequently. But instead of beating myself up I got back up and tried again. That means I spent most of my days trying again!

At some point I got the visual of when I learned to ride a bicycle for the first time. I recall how big that bicycle looked to me, and I knew I was choosing some scraped-up knees and elbows by trying to learn. But the damages would be worth the outcome, I was certain. In time I was able to ride that bicycle with style because I felt so "cool" for the accomplishment. Well, I wouldn't say the same about practicing the presence of God. But it is cool to have now practiced to the point that I can walk with Him step-by-step each day. In practicing a deeper awareness of His presence with me, I find myself closer and closer to the heart of God. I find His presence reassuring in whatever I find myself facing. He has provided this for us both. We can trust Him to have what we need before we ever ask for it from Him. I find it easier to face the hard things when my first thought is not the problem, but God's awaiting solution.

We can rely on God to show Himself faithful in all things. We are so prone to be self-reliant and yet God has called us to trust fully in Him. So, join with me and ask God what He would have you do. Talk to Him and wait on Him for the next step and direction to move in. See Him as the constant companion that He is to us as His children.

Perhaps it's a good time for you to join me on the path to practicing the presence of God in your own life. You will find God there. Start where you are and accept in advance that there will be some bumps and bruises along the way. You will find yourself in the constant presence of the Almighty if you continue. It doesn't get any better this side of heaven. Take that step closer to Him today and find Him present and able.

Dear Father,

We spend so much of our lives with other people and sometimes forget that You desire our time and connection to You the most. Thank You for making us aware that we need to walk with You constantly. Would You take us deeper into the awareness of Your presence today and help us to fix our eyes and hearts on practicing Your presence and relying fully on You?

Amen.

Psalm 46:7 Psalm 42:8 Exodus 4:12

Practicing the Presence of God
Psalm 143:8

1. Do you have an established time with God, on a regular basis, that is the only priority in that time?

2. Do you experience God's presence in your daily life? If not, how can you change that?

3. Look up the word "steadfast." Write down its meaning. Do you trust God's steadfast love?

4. How can you begin to practice the presence of God in your everyday life?

5. When a problem is before you, do you reach for God's available solution? Where do you find it?

Divine Appointments

"And he said to them, 'Go into all the world and proclaim the gospel to the whole creation.'"

Mark 16:15

I first heard the term "divine appointment" from my father. I actually used to get very frustrated when he would talk about a divine appointment that he had, but did not build it out. It left me thinking, what is he talking about? Now, here I am thirty years later having "divine appointments" often. So, what is a divine appointment?

These are the times when God brings something or someone into your path unexpectedly and He has a specific purpose for your meeting. This devotional could end up full of examples and yet my hope is not to so much give you examples as it is to equip you to see those moments, seize those moments, and use them for your own faith building.

Most people would not describe me as shy and that would be true. I was that person who wanted to help make the shy people feel more comfortable by being the one to speak up. Over the years I have had to grow in being willing to approach that one who doesn't have any "welcome" signs hanging around them. I've found that often that is the person I need to engage.

Let me share a recent example. I had gotten a manicure and a toe-polish change. This is a splurge that over eighteen years ago led me to a woman who became my sister in Christ. As we talked about Him for an hour every couple of weeks, I prayed as she shared with me about her life and practices of faith. Over time she saw her need for the one true God and became a Christian. She and I now refer to one another with the word "sister." We are good friends and sisters, way beyond her job. But that wasn't the divine appointment I was going to share with you, though it was one. I did not like the color on my toes recently, to the extent that I wanted to go get it changed. Did I mention that it gets harder to reach my toes every year?

I went to the shop, waited, and chatted with one of the employees while he was doing a lady's pedicure. Now, the lady in the chair seemed like the kind who was quiet and private. She did not say anything for a while, and then she began to join the conversation with a few comments. After I was done, I went over to the drying table, and she came a short while after. I engaged her, and little did I know where that would go. We talked about hard places in her life. She told me she was a Christian. Then shared that she was struggling with the idea of retirement that was coming, etc. Wow! We got in deep and quickly. It was rich and very enjoyable. I saw purpose all through our conversation and the leading of the Holy Spirit. At a point near our end, I told her, I don't think I came in here for a polish change. I think I had a "divine appointment" with you. She agreed.

As our conversation grew, she began to smile, and I could see that something I had said resonated with her. She needed to talk about exactly the things that we talked about that day. I needed to begin praying for Barbara in some specific ways and I told her that I would do so. I'm a firm believer that you don't tell someone that you will pray for them unless you fully intend to do it.

I sent Barbara a text that afternoon and told her how much I appreciated her openness with me and her willingness to be so transparent. She responded with a text telling me that this was not how she usually did things. In fact, at one point in our conversation, I recall her saying, I can't believe I'm telling you all of this. The good news was that she and I both understood that this was of God, and we went right to being comfortable with one another.

Barbara and I have continued to stay in touch via texts and I am still praying for the things she shared with me. What had to happen in order for this "divine appointment" to take place? First, it took me asking God to use me and lead me to those whom he had for me to engage with that day. I tell Him that I want Him to use me each day and then I ask Him to give me eyes to see what He has chosen for me as I go through it.

We have to be willing and ready to see the moments and appointments that God has prepared for us. That will only occur if we are connected to Him. We have to pursue Him and ask Him to lead us to these times. We then have to be on the lookout for them not only with our physical eyes but with the eyes of our spirit.

We have to be ready to seize those moments when God delivers them to us. I will say that one of the hardest things for me is that feeling I havc after I know that I missed a divine appointment. Yes, I am aware when the Holy Spirit is tapping me on the shoulder and I, for whatever reason, choose not to grab that golden opportunity before me. That can happen for a variety of reasons with me. But none of those reasons are ever enough to overcome the feeling of the lost opportunity. I know that God is using those times to show me just how valuable a "divine appointment" is when He offers it to me.

When a "divine appointment" comes to an end I have a feeling of contentment and I know it comes from God. It's like no other feeling. He will make up the time you give up, or the thing that you push back that you "think" you need to do instead. He knows that appointment is coming, and we must be willing to stop our motion and respond.

Why do we need "divine appointments?" We could look at them and say, other people need us, we want to look like Jesus to others, or even allow guilt or pressure to make us feel like we need to do something. None of these are the reason for a "divine appointment." I believe that God uses these moments not only for my good and the other person's good, but more importantly, He uses them to further His kingdom here on earth. When Jesus was preparing to leave the disciples and His followers to die on the cross for our sins, He told them to "go" and spread the gospel. How do we accomplish this in our daily lives apart from asking God to do it in us?

We must realize that God wants to grow our faith in Him as we follow Him daily. We aren't here just to make a plan and follow it until we meet the next day. No, I believe that He has the plan, and if we go to Him in order to ask for that plan, then we have to have the faith that He will do just that. He will make the way straight for us.

When He provides these appointments for us, I believe that He is waiting to see us respond in faith to Him, knowing that we don't have what it takes, but He does.

Like most things in life, the more we take on these divine appointments, the more we experience the work of God in and through us. We grow more willing, and perhaps even eager, to find that appointment along our way. I often think of these times like opening a surprise gift! I do love "good" surprises. I have come to know that these times are for me as much as for the other person, and God is growing me through these experiences as His daughter and follower. I want to grow and learn every day and I find that He never disappoints me because He is faithful.

So, where do you go from here as you enter this day? Are you asking God to give you these opportunities with others to further His kingdom and grow you more into His likeness? Today is a good day to take that step of faith and see what He might do with you and in you. What are you waiting for? Whatever it is I can promise you that it is not more valuable than the "divine appointment" that is awaiting you.

Dear God,

Thank You for continuing to teach me that my relationship with You is one that is living and active. I praise You for choosing to use me and grow me into a woman who looks like You through deeper faith in You. Thank You for the times You have gotten me beyond my comfort zone in order to take me to the places You wanted me to be. Give all of us greater faith, Lord, and a deeper determination to see You every single day.

Amen.

James 1:3 James 2:26 Hebrews 11:1

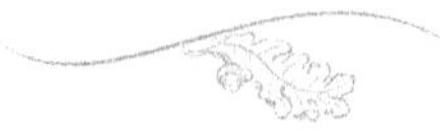

Divine Appointments
Mark 16:15

1. Can you recall a time when God specifically put you in someone else's presence with a purpose? Give an example.

2. When you look at others around you each day, do you see needs?

3. Are you available to God for divine appointments with others? If not, explain.

4. How will you ready yourself to meet the divine appointments God has for you?

5. What divine appointment have you experienced through someone else coming to you? What about the experience meant something special to you?

Hope Against Hope

"May the God of hope fill you with all joy and peace in believing, so that by the power of the Holy Spirit you may abound in hope."

Romans 15:13

There is an old song that contains a line that sticks in my head. It goes something like this: "Some days are diamonds, some days are stone, sometime the hard times won't leave me alone." I can't seem to forget the lyrics. I'd say it fits in the life that I live on a day-to-day basis.

It's not hard to say which type of day we would all choose if given the choice. I mean, women love diamonds, and well, that would just be an easy choice. However, we've all probably learned at this point that our days are not of our own choosing in type. We get to have the diamonds and stones all mixed up together.

I've been in a place I'm not very fond of lately. I'm in a tough situation, and my heart is all tied up in every aspect of it. I have a loved one who has distanced themselves greatly, and there is no open door at this time to walk through. I've sought God and His Word and know the "how tos" of going to her, and I have found that there is nothing to engage.

Some days I wake up and know the tears are coming and that they may last all day beneath the surface of my exterior. Other days I find myself hopeful in God and trusting that He is working through all of these things even though I can't see, hear, taste, or smell Him. How do we stay hopeful on those days until another diamond day arrives at our door?

Let me say first that I fully believe that God has purpose in those stone days. If I take Him at His word then I know that He is growing my faith, deepening my trust in Him, shaping me more into His image, and strengthening me for greater battles. I need all of those things; we all do. But getting to them never seems to be enjoyable though they are necessary. I believe that my struggles are from God and He knows what He is doing in me, as He did with David in the Psalms. It's okay for me to struggle, to grieve, to cry out to Him and repeatedly tell Him, "I don't know how to do this!" He can handle all of those things from me and you and welcomes us to bring them to Him.

How do we stay hopeful? I think it is crucial that we look backward in our lives and see where God has met us in the past. We need to search for those times when He has been ever faithful to us. For me, this drives my thoughts to a focused place and my perspective shifts toward hope once again. It's also important to take hold of God's Word and read it. Most of us own the Bible and yet how often do we grab hold of it when we are hurting and hopeless? I am thinking our first reach is more likely to be for those cookies or that ice cream. But they will only make us feel worse about our decision later on. If we would reach for God's words and search for His promises to us we would never fall short of comfort, compassion, love, truth, or hope.

It's also going to be necessary to practice this over and over. Satan loves to sink our hearts through unproductive thoughts that he plants in our minds, which only stir our struggles. A fine older woman once told me in love, "Honey, the battles are won and lost between your two ears." Think about that. Our thinking has everything to do with our choosing how we will see things on any given day. We can choose to stay in the struggle or we can ask God to take our thinking to a higher place of hope and promise. It really is up to us. God is always ready to meet us where we are.

There will be times for all of us when we just need to shed some tears, grieve, and find our limits and His beginnings. God understands all of this. I take comfort in the realization that He is there to hold me on those days and walk along with me in that place. Besides, all of those tears are being saved up in heaven and one day there will be no more tears. Praise God! I'm all-in for that day.

It's a good day to check on that hope you've been given as a God girl. Open His Word and look for what He has already provided for you as you journey through this day. He doesn't expect us to have it all in place. He gives the days and provides His Spirit in us to go through them with us. Choose to find your hope today in Christ and hey, make it a great day.

Dear Father,

It is truly difficult to stay focused on what I know to be best practice for me. Hope can seem so small when despair is in my face. Thank You for going ahead of us and providing Your Word to accompany us through this lifetime. You planned all of our days and You've graciously given us all that we need. Help us to live in light of that today.

Amen.

Joshua 4:2-7 Jeremiah 29:13 Philippians 4:19

Hope Against Hope
Romans 15:13

1. How do you stay hopeful when you are in a day that is a "stone"?

2. Do you take your weakness to God and tell Him what you feel? Take a minute to write out a weakness to Him.

3. Write down an example of a time in the past when God met you in your circumstances despite your lack of hope.

4. Has God been faithful to you?

5. How can you daily bring hope into your thinking and remind yourself that God is not done?

Kindness

"Be kind to one another, tenderhearted, forgiving one another, as God in Christ forgave you."

Ephesians 4:32

In these days that we are living in, we have heard a great deal about anger and kindness. The word "kind" has become a buzzword and is printed on signs, t-shirts, and in a variety of forms of display. Some of these displays seem to be rooted in true kindness but others feel like they are there to create a sense of guilt and inaccurate self-reflections.

I have spent some time contemplating the word "kindness," which led me to scripture. It also landed me in some deep inner searching over messages that are perhaps not created to further true kindness.

We are told in Ephesians 4:32 to "be kind to one another." This is a good starting place for us. Why are we to be kind to each other? Because God has told us to do so. At times I find it incredibly hard to be kind toward someone when I am not feeling love toward them. I tend to take the duck-and-cover mentality. What does that look like? I withdraw and keep silent until the situation is over. In my lifetime I have been through some very hurtful and threatening things. Maybe you have too.

How are we to then be kind to others, all others? If we look at Galatians 5:22-23 we will find the fruits of the Spirit that come from Christ living in us include kindness and love. That means they exist in me at all times through the Holy Spirit. Does that mean they pop up when I need them most? No, it means they are at my disposal, and it is up to me to choose to access them. These fruits were put in me when I became God's child. So, how do I activate this kindness when I don't feel like being kind?

We can both do so if we recall the kindness that God has shown us already through Christ's death for us, His creation of the world for us, and His choice to love us first, before we loved Him. He is the example that we are to follow. There will be times when we don't feel remotely inspired to show kindness and yet the ability to be kind is there, inside us. Perhaps it's hidden behind our anger, hurt feelings, selfishness, or defensiveness. If this is the case then we have some work to do in order to get our "stuff" out of the way so that God can do His stuff.

I recall a time when someone sent me a very intentional, ugly, lengthy text while I was headed out of town on vacation. I knew before I ever opened the text that this was a flaming spear. It was aimed toward my heart, and it was straight from Satan's bow. I told my husband that the text was there and that unless he disagreed, I was not going to open it until we were headed home. We agreed that this was the best practice at the time.

As we were driving home, I opened the text and read it aloud so that we could hear it at the same time. We quickly identified what the purpose of the text might be, and we discussed what we were feeling in response. Because we had put this aside and let it sit, it had no power over us. When we did approach it, we were much better equipped to respond rather than react. Did I feel like being kind to the sender? Absolutely not. After about two weeks of praying, letting it rest, and discussing it with my husband, I felt compelled to contact the sender and ask them to come over to our home and discuss the text, as well as where we were as believers.

We did get together and two hours after we'd begun, we finished. I asked the sender, what was really going on when you sent that text to me? What were you really feeling? It took a while to get the conversation flowing, but we got there. In the end we had agreed over the fact that Satan would love to use these things to destroy an otherwise good relationship that we had been enjoying.

But we'd have never gotten there if I had not reached within myself, past the anger and hurt, to beyond myself. It took me letting go of what I felt temporarily to reach for the kindness that I had within me from God. I knew that I was not denying myself anything. What I was doing was going beyond myself to reach to this one who mattered to me. In doing so I was trusting God to protect my feelings and my total well-being in this act of faith. God alone could take me through this and land me safely on the other side. And that is exactly what He did. The outcome was a desirable one but even if it had not been, it was up to me to show kindness toward the one who had offended me.

I can tell you that this is one of the hardest things for me to do. My flesh just rises up in opposition to this way of doing things. When I think about that strong feeling within myself, I begin to see just how very kind God has been to my ugly, rebellious heart. I have tested Him time and time again and yet He has remained kind toward me. I think also about Jesus and how people treated Him. He was guilty of nothing and yet He was killed for crimes he never committed. He took the burden of my unkind heart and yours and removed them through His death on the cross.

So, how hard is it to get past our own feelings to find the God-given kindness that He has planted within us when we are in a hard place? There will certainly be some places that can take a long time to get past, and we can trust Him with the timing of all of these things. Through every experience God leads us through, we will become more aware of our need to look to Him, to call Him, and to more fully understand how to apply His kindness. Ultimately, it is our choice to be like Him through kindness. In and of ourselves, we would choose differently. As we take every thought captive and seize the opportunities that God gives us we will find that kindness more easily accessible.

If we truly want to understand what it means to be kind, we don't have to look far. God is kind; He gives kindness to us. He can get us past ourselves to give us full access to His kindness. We just have to be willing to seek Him in all things.

Dear Father,

Thank You for seeing my need long before I often do. You have demonstrated such kindness to us as Your children, and we don't want to keep that to ourselves. Help us when we don't feel kind to reach beyond our feelings to find Your kindness. Help us to be true to You and to ourselves as we seek to share Your kindness with others.

Amen.

Galatians 5:22-23 1 Corinthians 13:4
Romans 11:22.

Kindness
Ephesians 4:32

1. What in Christ's example to us gives us reason to be kind?

2. Has God placed kindness in you, or is it something you have to work up within yourself? Read Galatians 5:22-23. What do you see in these verses?

3. Do you have a good friend to whom you take your choices to seek her help and hold you accountable? Why would this be important?

4. What can we expect from God when we choose to respond in kindness rather than out of our pain?

5. How should you deal with feelings of hurt that remain, or linger, toward one who has offended you?

Time for an Update

*"For we are his workmanship,
created in Christ Jesus for good works,
which God prepared beforehand,
that we should walk in them."*

Ephesians 2:10

Do you enjoy a good renovation program on television as much as I do? I'm pretty sure that I went through every episode of one show just riding the bike and rowing at the gym. I'm not sure what it is about these shows, but I can shoot thirty minutes easily while working out by watching them. I also amped up on them a few years before we started some home renovations. What is it about making something over into something better that we love so much?

I can't say the same thing when the renovation is being done to me. God has taken many of the things that needed reconstruction in my heart and worked them over until they looked totally different. I'm pretty sure I've had some total overhauls done; you know, the kind where we are talking taking that room down to the studs!

What did I learn about renovation through my own journey of a few bathrooms and a kitchen? I learned that renovations take longer than you think they will, they don't go smoothly, there are lots of surprises that may delay the process, they take a lot out of you, and sometimes you don't like the end result.

In my mind, I compared the work done in my home and in my heart when I recently read this verse in Ephesians. One strong comparison that came to me was that, in the end, things look much better, and what was, is no more. This is a good picture of what God does when we ask Christ into our hearts. We really have no idea of the amount of work that God has intended for our lives.

Jesus had a plan all along to reconcile me to Himself, redeem me from my sin, and renovate my heart of flesh into His likeness. When we invite Him to be our Savior, He brings His plans with Him, and we go under construction. He patiently toils to reconstruct our thinking, acting, and expressions. The good news is that He only creates masterpieces. If we can endure the process of our transformation, we will, in time, be complete in Christ.

We have to begin by recognizing that despite our sin, Jesus desires us and loves us despite His sinlessness. How many people do you know who see you this way? I think I know that number without asking. If He has no sin, then why would He ever entertain me, as full of sin as I am? I feel sure that I can sin in my mind in less than ten seconds. Satan just loves to work on my mind. And yet, Christ still bids me to come to Him. This is love.

Not only did He love us, but He knew that we would never be freed from all our thoughts and actions that condemn us daily. So, He went the distance for you and me. He went all the way to the cross to buy us back to Himself. He loved us enough to redeem us through His own sinless death. When was the last time anyone even stopped at a store entrance to let you go in first? We are walking in a time when things all seem to be focused on ourselves. If Christ had been like us, then we would never have known redemption power.

Upon entry into our hearts, He begins bringing in the big equipment and has a dumpster delivered for our driveways. And though there might be some really big work to be done, He is gentle, timely, patient, and creative. He was a woodworker when He lived on the Earth, so I tend to think that He only does amazing work!

Perhaps the hardest part for all of us in these overhauls is trusting that He is working toward something great in us. We have to participate in this work. If we resist the work, then it will take much longer than planned. If we change our minds about being on board, then the construction may come to a standstill. If we need to become more patient with the process, then we might find that the materials that are needed are on back order and will take much longer than anyone planned.

So, how do we continue through the process of Jesus renovating our hearts into the places that best reflect His glory and likeness? My answer would be to stay close to your Master Contractor and His plan that is ours in the Bible. Stay in regular communication with Him. Be prepared to struggle along the way, knowing that the outcome will far exceed your greatest imaginings. He has the plan, and once He gets started in us, we must desire that He continues in all circumstances.

The thing is, when Christ is doing the work, it is always best! He does His work with love and patience, kindness, gentleness, grace, and purpose. There will not be any do-overs, hopefully. Remember, we have to accept the changes and learn to enjoy them throughout all of our days. May we both yield to the work that He longs to do in us and may we resemble Him to others all the days of our lives.

Dear Jesus,

Thank You for always wanting what is best for me even when I don't like the way it feels or looks. Thank You for gently reminding me that my life is not my own. Have Your way in me, Master, and create in me a clean heart and desire for more of You. I desire Your work, Lord. Make me brave to embrace every calling that You desire through me and make me into Your likeness through them all.

Amen.

Galatians 2:20 Romans 5:10 Psalm 51:10

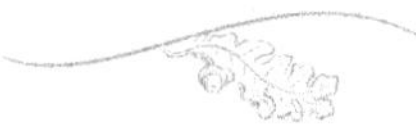

Time for an Update
Ephesians 2:10

1. Describe the update that God did in your life when you accepted Him as your Savior.

2. How is God working currently to change your heart and make it more like His?

3. Are you standing in the way of a change that God wants to bring in you? If so, what is it that He wants to update?

4. Are you working with God to bring about a new and transformed you? What has it required of you?

5. Is your goal to look like Christ to the world around you?

Enduring Friendship

"Two are better than one, because they have a good reward for their toil."

Ecclesiastes 4:9

If you have been a Christian for any length of time you have probably heard about Jonathan and David. They shared a relationship that stands out through its testing and trying. Theirs is a picture of friend love. Though they were not family, they were deeply close friends. Their relationship was a long-haul one.

Do you have a lifelong friend who has walked alongside you in good times and bad? One whom you've committed your attention and time to? Some of us do get long-haul friends who continue for decades. And others of us get seasons with a precious one, for one reason or another.

I have a dear friend who is what I would refer to as "tried and true." Her life began in a very committed family that loved her dearly. They worked hard at things, but most of all they worked at loving one another. She has truly carried on that legacy of love with many friends and acquaintances, as well as with her family. I recall when she was in college how her father would send her a roll of stamps because she was the card-sending queen! He loved her by feeding her love for others. She is the one who shows up when it matters most. I'd say she is one person I know who is there for others with her loving presence and strong quietness in most all circumstances.

I, on the other hand, was not raised in a home where love was demonstrated like this and I recall how foreign it was to me when her family was simply there for one another. I had not had the same example of love and devotion. I found many years after leaving home that I did not know how to be a loving and committed friend, but I desperately wanted to learn how. I had friends growing up, but I did not know how to go deep with them.

For me this was a real struggle. But this friend I've spoken of has taught me much in my sixty-three years about how to be a good friend through the distance of time. There was a time when we lived together, and we were like bookends. We were the opposite of one another, and it worked for us. We'd studied the same area of learning in college and so our lives overlapped much of the time.

After college we went in different directions to use our teaching degrees to further learning with special-education students. We were passionate and eager; oh, to be twenty-one again! As time passed in our different worlds we stayed in touch, but life took over.

I ended up getting married and she was my maid of honor. She was the one who knew me best, next to my husband. Not long after that I started having children and my priorities shifted. Life just has a way of doing that. She was the stability pillar in my hometown. When my family went home to visit the two sets of grandparents it was hard to a find time for a visit. She always went the distance to make it happen. She was and is a good friend.

My children began to grow up and it grew more challenging to stay in touch as regularly, and yet this dear friend continued to send birthday, anniversary, Christmas, and a variety of other holiday cards to me. She was faithful. Honestly, there were times when I felt like a failure to her, and yet my heart loved her. She loved me through first birthdays, a horrible divorce, and the death of both of my parents. She has been a faithful friend.

This friend has shown me a very vivid picture of what the love of Christ looks like. Often, it has been thoughts of her that have driven my actions toward others in committed love. Like Jonathan and David, she lives a love that is steady and sure. I long to be that friend to others each and every day, and I thank God for keeping her in my view to show me how. I know that I am still learning from her, and I hope to for at least a few more decades. Even if we begin our lives not knowing how to do something, we still have the opportunity to learn. God is teaching us daily what it means to be more like Him, if we are seeking His will and perfect ways in ourselves. He knows that we will fall short, and His forgiveness is great.

God designed each of us to need relationship with one another and it is up to us to pursue those relationships. Don't let go of those relationships that may drift at times. Perhaps we don't know why their course has drifted from ours, but we can rest assured that God begins and finishes all of His work in us. We can trust Him for what lies ahead, and we can continue to pursue loving, committed relationships that are rooted in Christ.

Dear Father,

Thank You for using everything that we encounter to teach us of Your nature and being. Thank You for designing us for relationship and seeing that we grasp that design through Your purposeful means. Thank You for the picture of love you have given me through this precious woman whom we both love. Bless those who love us, and give us the time to love them more.

Amen.

1 Samuel 20:17 1 Samuel 20:23 Proverbs 18:24

Enduring Friendship

Ecclesiastes 4:9

1. Do you have a tried-and-true friend? If so, who is she and why would you describe her as your "tried and true friend"?

2. How has your growing up shaped your friendship relationships with others?

3. Is there a friend whom God might be calling you to go deeper with in relationship and accountability?

4. What qualities do you find valuable in a "good friend"?

5. What would your true friend say are some qualities that she values in you?

Right Thinking

"Turn away from evil and do good; seek peace and pursue it."

Psalm 34:14

What brings you down, saps you, and takes your mind to a place that is dim? We are living in a day and time when there is much to be discouraged by if we are depending on our physical eyes and ears. The news surrounding us remain discouraging and, unfortunately, there are many who seek to dwell on the dark side as they engage one another. The comments around us are a swirl of negativism, pessimism, doom, and gloom. Yes, these are dark times and yet how long can any of us as believers allow these types of thoughts to dwell in our hearts and minds?

Someone close in my life shared a situation with me recently about an individual whom they are having to interface with on a regular basis. They described this individual as the "most negative" person they've ever met. Not exactly the title any of us in Christ should be desirous of receiving. This idea really stuck in my thinking as I began to pray for the situation and the position of my friend. The person we are referring to would readily tell you that they are a Christian. That further influenced my thinking.

We have to ask ourselves some valuable questions when we interface with fellow believers in Christ who are fixed on negative thinking. It is a slippery slope for sure. We can begin to buy into this thinking with them or we can fix our eyes on things above as God has told us to do. We do have a choice. The question is, do we make a choice for a different tact, or join in for the sake of conversation and lack of ability to stand on God's truth?

We are being told these days that we need to accept everyone's perspective or we are being negative. Not true. Our thinking isn't to be based on man's measures, but on God's standard. When you are talking about a fellow believer, how do you respond in love to those negative perspectives, that bring both of you further down?

Our starting point has to be "right thinking." Where do we get this? In God's Word, the Bible. If we desire to live in Him, then we have to know what He has told us to do and how we are to do it. We have to prioritize time in God's Word so that we know how to respond before we get into that situation where we will need it. Next, we have to be willing to stand on the truths that we know. When the conversation begins to turn south, we have to be willing to point north with our words.

What we say and do must look different than the downward-focused comments and thinking. I'm not suggesting that we need only to be positive and cheery. I am suggesting that we have to be willing to say to that person, is there another way to see this? We have to be willing, in love, to help turn that person's thinking in a Christ-centered direction. Yes, it may take many attempts to get that individual to shift their negative thinking. If you are going to be in their presence regularly, then you are going to need perseverance and lots of right thinking.

You may never turn this bottom-dweller into a heavenward visionary, but you will have an impact if you have right thought and love to guide this person to the same. Above all, pray for this one to see that they are stuck in a pattern of negativism. Negativism just multiplies upon itself and after a while they will find themselves talking to themselves because others have drifted away. God's purpose is to unite us and use us to lift one another up to His perspective and truth.

So, when you are tempted to jump in with someone's negative thoughts, take a moment and consider the choice that you have before you speak. Where would God want this to go for you both? At times we may have to walk away. But more often than not, we can walk into this place and bring different thinking through Christ. Pray, persist, practice right thinking, and be prepared to speak the truth in love today.

Father,

We are often tempted to jump into the dirty places with others and once we get in, it is hard to get back out. Would You give us the foresight to see that the time for us to get ready for these types of situations is before we get there? Help our thinking and our words to glorify You in all that we say, all that we do. There is much opposition to right thinking these days and yet it is what You call me to. Help me to stand for what is right and good in You.

Amen.

Psalm 37:27 Proverbs 4:15 Proverbs 14:16

Right Thinking
Psalm 34:14

1. Do you find yourself buying into negative thinking through comments of others? How does this leave you feeling?

2. What is one thing you've learned from God's Word that helps you have right thinking?

3. Are you called to change other people's thinking? Or, are we called to stand on God's truth?

4. Do you pray for God to show you how to have right thinking? Write out a short prayer to God.

5. Are you seeking peace through right thinking rather than through the approval of others? If so, describe.

Throne Moments

"We do not have a high priest who is unable to empathize with our weakness, but we have one who has been tempted in every way, just as we are—yet he did not sin. Let us then approach God's throne of grace with confidence, so that we may receive mercy and find grace to help us in our time of need."

Hebrews 4:15-16 NIV, ESV, NKJV

Where do your thoughts go first when you are struggling over an issue? When I read these verses, it seems so very clear that I need to see Jesus first. Isn't it good news to know that He can empathize with us? I know that when I am struggling with an ongoing problem, I am prone to call one of my girlfriends and vent with her. They love Jesus too, and they help me defuse the situation oftentimes. But I can forget that Jesus Himself has known what I am now knowing as a struggle. These verses even spell out that He "was tempted in every way, just as we are."

This puts a framework on the realities of my struggles. I am not alone, and Jesus understands. At times it feels like one struggle doesn't end without another one popping up. It is kind of like that Whac-A-Mole game. I find that when things are in this kind of flow that it is extra hard for me to stay focused on God. Recently I was in a Sunday school class and the teacher was speaking on the armor of God. He challenged us to take one piece of the armor and apply it to our lives differently as a result of the lesson. I knew right away that my need was to spend time on the "helmet of salvation" (Ephesians 6:17).

He had used an illustration that really stuck with me that day and I chose to apply this armor a little more intentionally each day after that. Here is why: I can't very well do much else until I understand that my mind is a battlefield. I began to look at how well I was applying the protection offered me through the helmet. He had shown us a helmet of a Roman soldier. It had guards to the side of each eye. At that point I thought about how the soldier could only see straight in front of him. His peripheral vision was basically nonexistent.

It was very convicting for me at this point because my vision can look like hash browns at Waffle House most of the time, smothered and scattered. I don't even have to try to get distracted; it comes very easily. The scripture tells us to guard our mind and to focus it, on things above. And yet, Satan loves to undo my right thoughts faster than I can attach to them. It is frustrating, to say the least.

These verses remind me that this level of temptation from the Enemy is not unfamiliar to Him at all. And God loves us so much that He gave us steps to help us stay on the foundation that will not be moved. We are to start by "approaching the throne of grace with confidence." That's good news, and not difficult to do. Go to God who sits on the throne of grace and go with certainty in Him. Most of the time I realize I have no ability to change these thoughts that are seeking to undo me, and my confidence is poor. However, when I remember that my confidence is not in myself, but in Christ alone, I get moving toward the throne.

Next, the reason to approach His throne of grace is given to us, "so that we may receive mercy and grace to help us in our time of need." With this image of God in my mind I see a loving and open-armed Father who is ready to meet me in my need. Notice, I didn't say "meet my need," but rather, "in my time of need." He is already awaiting my inabilities, with His ability. I love the fact that God is so very intentional in all of His ways. He is ready to hear from us even if we have failed one hundred times before.

In my own thinking it is very easy to see things in light of my fleshly ability to conquer things and yet He does not need my help. He invites us to come to Him, in order that He can graciously meet us there in our need. Are your struggles at times trivial in your mind, or do you think that

God doesn't need to be bothered with them? You couldn't be farther from the truth. He is here for just that purpose.

So, when you are sitting in traffic, and you left your last gram of patience at work, is this a throne moment? Is it worth asking God to help you in the weakness of your patience? Oh yes, it is! When you are standing in a restaurant with a menu that contains every single thing you want and you know that only one is a good choice for you, is that a throne moment? What about when your husband comes home in a bad mood for the third day and you are personally not wanting to address that mood, is that a throne moment? Indeed, these are all throne moments. When we need help, we are absolutely in a throne moment.

Stop the chaos in your mind long enough to go to God and see that He awaits you with mercy and grace to help you in that time of need. I think at times God must get weary with me because I am always at that throne asking for help. But are we going to take Him at His word or not? He has offered and is ready; we have to go and take that need to Him. We must activate that faith in Him and see Jesus who was tempted just as we are. He identifies with you. So, grab some of that confidence that comes from all of the times that He has met you in the past and go to the Father's throne.

Dear Father,

Thank You for the image of You as being our father. These words from Your Word are so tender, so personal. You knew that we could never identify with Christ if we didn't have His earthly life as an example that we could relate to. How good You are to love us as You do. Thank you for the mercy and grace that is there, awaiting us at Your throne every minute of every day. Help us to fix our eyes on You and accept that presence that You offer us in all times. We need You and You knew we would. Thank you, Father.

Amen.

Colossians 3:2 1 Corinthians 15:57 Hebrews 12:28

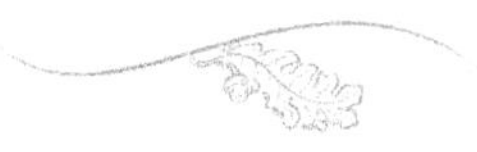

Throne Moments
Hebrews 4:15-16

1. Would you say that Jesus is your best friend? Do you see your relationship with Him as being one of "best friends"?

2. Do you take time to consider how Jesus identifies with your struggles and sufferings? What have you learned from doing this?

3. What does Hebrews 4:15 have to say to us when we are in a place of need?

4. Describe a throne moment you've experienced recently. What brought you to the throne?

5. Does God want you to come to Him in the "moments" of your life? Is anything unimportant to God in regard to you?

Keeping Our Perspective

"Only let your manner of life be worthy of the gospel of Christ, so that whether I come and see you or am absent, I may hear of you that you are standing firm in one spirit, with one mind striving side by side for the faith of the gospel."

Philippians 1:27

When you wake up in the morning, what is your first thought? Think about that for a minute. Do you awaken with a thousand thoughts running through your mind? Do you just focus hard on not stumbling as you get up because your body is moving but your brain has not joined it? I understand if the above are your tendencies.

Trusting our minds to put us in the right place is actually a dangerous way to begin our days. At times I have to immediately begin thanking God for anything and everything that comes to mind, in order to ward off the Enemy's thoughts that are ready to implant in my brain before I'm fully awake. Satan would love to take us rapidly down the path to a terrible, horrible, no good, very bad day.

However, if we are God girls then we have to be ready to call on Jesus before our heads leave the pillow. These are the moments that set the tone for every step that we will potentially take. I don't know about you, but I can literally be tempted to sin several times before I ever leave my bedroom. Our minds are a gateway to wrong thinking, focus, and follow-through.

We can quickly lose perspective through wrong thinking. Tell me you have those days where you have gotten mad, and you can't even remember what made you mad. Perhaps this is not a struggle for you, and you wake up each day with a thankful thought. But for me this is game-on time, and I am very aware of it.

Have you seen the signs that say, "If mama ain't happy, ain't nobody happy?" Well, that may be tongue-in-cheek joking, but it also bears a lot of truth. We as women often set the tone not only for ourselves, but for our husbands and household. Where we put our perspective can definitely bleed over into the lives of those we love and ruin their days, as well as ours.

That causes me to ask myself daily, where is my perspective? If we have the right thinking, then we are more apt to have the right actions. So, how do we set our perspectives in the right place and sustain them there? First ,we have to know the truth so that we can identify a lie. For example, you rise, look in your bathroom mirror, and think to yourself, I look horrible. Those wrinkles are growing every day. I don't want to age. Gosh, what will I look like in five more years? If it's this bad now, I mean, what will five more years look like? That's about 1,825 days! That's definitely going to show.

Before we know it we are seeing things in a perspective. Is it a true view, or is it one tainted by the expectations of this world and not God's pure perspective? He has told us how He loves us and claims us as we are, period. He has made us beautiful in His timing. If we begin by diminishing that perspective, then where do you think our day will go from there?

We really don't want to give that steering wheel over to the Enemy of our souls that quickly, do we? I believe that we must start with the truth and keep telling ourselves the truth throughout the challenges of every given day. Besides, Satan is all about selling us lies; it is his specialty. Why buy them readily? In order to right our perspective and ongoing thinking we have to look to God who authored our days and will perfect them in time. We have a role in this, and it requires us to respond with the truth of God's Word.

In order to be readied we have to spend time with God in His Word, the Bible. If we seek that truth before we need of it, we will be equipped when things start heading off track for us. If we were going on a hike, we would prepare ahead by making sure we had water, a snack, communication access, and some form of protection. Why would we prepare any less readily for the enemy of our souls and the impact we will have on those who are nearest to us?

I've often told my daughters, if you fail to plan, you plan to fail. I am certain that probably irritated them on some level. But think about it. We have been given tools through God's Word to help us navigate our paths. The alternate instead always brings a range of emotions with it. When things go wrong, and they will, we find out what our true strength of spirit really is. I personally don't like dealing with the fallout on the flip side. I find recovery just seems to be so much harder. We are all different and my household is a testimony to that truth.

God longs to further our days with the things He has for us, and some days we may have to do some serious battle to get beyond Satan to arrive at God's best. That's the battle I want to be equipped for. Maybe that is due to years of battle and challenged thinking. But my word to you, as well as myself today, is let's begin the days we are given by setting our minds on things above. Take God's Word and let it be your sword against the perspective robber.

Dear Father,

It is so easy to fall into the traps that Satan prepares for us as we begin each day with You. Help us, Lord, to hide Your words in our hearts and apply it when he seeks to undermine Your truth in us. We need You, Lord, to champion our hearts each day and fit us for the battles. We love You, Lord, and long to do Your will alone.

Amen.

Colossians 3:2 Ecclesiastes 3:11 Hebrews 12:2

Keeping Our Perspective
Philippians 1:27

1. How do you set your perspective in the right place and sustain it? Explain.

2. What gets you to a terrible, horrible, no good, very bad day place? List a few ideas.

3. Do you identify these thoughts that tend to derail you and turn them over to God for help? How?

4. What truths from God's Word do you keep in your arsenal to do battle against the Enemy with?

5. What do you want to give to the others who live with you each day through your perspective? How will you achieve that? Describe.

Through the Journey

"Rejoice in hope, be patient in tribulation, be constant in prayer."

Romans 12:12

So often in life we are going through something, coming into something, or coming out of something. Much of our time is spent in motion. Isn't it good to know that no matter what we are going through that God has specifically told us what position we need to take? We need some hope, some patience, and lots of prayer.

This verse reminds me of many of the harder times in life that I have walked through. It also takes me to where God met me in all of those times. Somehow, He kept my eyes focused on Him, and brought me to the other side of each experience with hope. He alone can get the credit in my life for that truth.

When we are surrounded with hard times, that is the best time to look for where God is in our circumstances. It is often not our first thought, but it is the best thought we can embrace. It takes our eyes off our situation and puts them where they belong, on Him. I wish I could tell you that I have developed a button within myself that automatically takes me to that place in every challenge, but that is not true. Like you, I have to make daily a decision to arrive at that kind of thinking.

I had a daughter who was born with a heart defect twenty-nine years ago. I had already become a mother twice, but this one, she came in a different way. When I delivered her, they did not put her up on my chest. Instead, people were moving quickly, and I could not see my doctor's face to determine if we were okay. In the moments after, I learned that she had come out very purple and they were working to get her breathing and responding. She rallied and the worst was past us.

However, this was a beginning to a road that would not leave us. On day two of life, we went for multiple testing. During the testing I could not touch her, nurse her, comfort her, or pacify her. She just wailed and I produced fear at record speed. It was tough. I can't tell you that my first thought was God, but I did call out to Him in those desperate times of great fear. In those moments I needed the hope God has promised us.

We learned that the problem our daughter had would be manageable over her lifetime, however, we would not know the extent of the problem until she had matured to around two years of age. The road looked really long! I can say that I did not parent her the same as I had my other two children. I took every moment as one that was a gift that might be gone at some point. Though nothing was leaning that way, this was my thinking.

Don't get me wrong, I loved and delighted myself with my other children, but I lived my days and nights with an extra measure of caution and attention over this one. At the time, I felt ongoing tribulation in my heart and mind. "What ifs" just came way too easily when things got quiet.

Over time I learned that I needed the words of Philippians 4:8 to help me focus beyond the moments of my worries and refocus me on what God had for me. The verse tells us to focus on "whatever is true, honorable, just, pure, lovely, commendable, excellent, and worthy of praise." That put things into perspective for me. My worries were not any of those things. I had to take each one and exchange them for the "greater" thoughts that God had laid out for me.

The truth was, I had today with this child and really, she was never mine. God made her and she belonged to Him. He had just chosen to share her with me for the time He deemed good. I continued to find right thinking through this verse, and I intentionally sought to apply the words to my moment-by-moment thinking. My worries decreased and my hope and prayer life began to grow.

In the early days I found myself asking God, why does this have to be the case? Why can't she just be healthy like the other girls? God gently reminded me that His thoughts were not my thoughts, and His ways were not my ways. I began to see myself as one who is here to fulfill His thoughts and ways and not my own. I realized that I had to fully give this child back to Him, trusting that He would do all His holy will, and I would arrive safely on the other side of this challenge. If I allowed this challenge to overtake my thinking, I would surely drown in sorrow and worry. But God has a plan, and it does not include us living in either.

That daughter is now twenty-nine and is carrying her third child as I write this. She has two healthy children and a healthy life, with the heart problem. How good is God? Very, very good. I know that not all outcomes are met with good endings. I have had several of those too, in other ways. But this time, God was teaching me to trust Him for the plans that He had for both of us.

So, remember today that it is always best to pause when the challenges come and check to see where God is in your thinking and in your current situation. Find that hope that only He can give you. Be patient while He is working through the tribulations of your life and pray continually. He is always listening and ready to hear from you. He has the things we desire (from Him) and He wants us to bring our problems to Him. Then look within your own heart and find that thing in your circumstances that is "worthy of praise" (Philippians 4:8). Start singing in praise to God for the good things that He has done. Finally, trust Him for what is still ahead in what you are going through. He will complete all of His holy will.

Dear Father,

Those days I walked through with You are still so vivid. During the experience I did not see how You were going to take care of this child, but You were constantly calling me to fix my eyes on You. Thank You. Your thoughts and ways are what I want to live in light of each and every day. Go before me today, Father, and teach me to continue through every path You lead me to. For I know that You will lead me down it too.

Amen.

Isaiah 43:2 Philippians 4:8 Isaiah 55:8

Through the Journey
Romans 12:12

1. What do we need most when we are going through a rough time?

2. When there is nothing that you can do to change things, how do you continue? Give a personal example.

3. When you worry, how can Philippians 4:8 help you? Give an example.

4. Is there something you are struggling to trust God fully with? Write a prayer to God about it.

5. How can you help yourself see the good even in what feels bad? God is there in those times too. What can you remind yourself of in these times?

Living in This Day

*"This is the day that the LORD has made;
let us rejoice and be glad in it."*

Psalm 118:24

If you woke today knowing that this would be your last day on earth, what would you do on this last day? We'd probably do everything we could to make every moment count, not letting even one slip away. I also imagine that we would think quickly about what things were priorities and what things did not matter. We could chop off many things from our "to-do list" and carefully choose how to refill it with necessity.

Perhaps we would find ourselves in the middle of the most intentional day of our lives. I think that sometimes life is more easily lived with known limitations than freedoms. This thinking would surely shift the way we would spend that last day. My point is that we can tend to live life in a cycle of putting things off that we know are priorities in order to grab some time for freedom of mind. How often do we say, I need to do such and such, I should do that today, I could do that task today, but I think I'll wait until later. We all have done this at some point, and maybe there are those of us who have learned to practice a life of putting things off only to end up frustrated with ourselves later down the road.

Our world has us all living in a setting of "fast." It seeps into every area of our lives until anything that requires us to slow down causes immediate frustration. All we have to do is look around us to see examples without end.

This past week my husband and I were away for a week of vacation. Our minds were definitely in the "pause mode." We sat for many days at the surf and watched the tides roll in and then back out again. One of our days away began and ended with rain, heavy rain. The kind that the umbrella really doesn't help with. Like most tourists and perhaps residents, we decided to go shopping. We were nice and soggy by the end of our time out.

During our adventures we were readying to cross a drive that led to a parking lot. The car nearest us stopped to let us cross. However, the car behind it decided that they couldn't wait for them to move again so they decided to pass the stilled car. My husband and I were halfway through the lanes when the car plowed toward us. The driver then floored her horn and started yelling with her words and hands.

She slowed down a bit, but she moved right on through, taking her impatience with her. A couple in the lot came over to us to tell us they'd seen the entire thing and checked to see if we were okay. As we crawled into our vehicle the conversation began with a question. What is more important than stopping for a pedestrian who has the right of way?

You see, I have actually been hit twice, yes, twice by a car while on foot in a parking lot. I guess I'm just lucky that way. But seriously, what is the rush? How have we allowed ourselves to get to the point that we rush through life and overlook the value of our days and the lives of others? Have we completely forgotten that God has given a numbered set of days and that He has plans for each and every one of them? Are we trusting Him with the timing of those days or are we busying ourselves through them in an effort to get more time for "me"?

How much rejoicing would there have been if the impatient driver had hit both my husband and me? Would excuses have flown from her mouth the moment she exited her vehicle? What was most important in those moments? I can look at her and condemn her very easily for her impatient choices and yet I'd also have to look at myself and say, guilty. We are so prone to spend our days in that rush and yet, God has not called us to rush. He tells us to wait on Him, to rest in His timing and to not trust in our own inabilities in order to find His perfect ways.

He has told us to "rejoice" in this day. I don't know about you, but I can't rejoice when I am griping about something that I can't do anything about. So, in those moments of that parking lot, I determined to thank God and rejoice. I rejoiced over our continued life in this world with one another. I thanked God for always going before us and behind us. I rejoiced over the ability not to hold this lady's actions against her and I got to choose not to lose the rest of the day God had given us to upset thoughts about what "could" have happened. We chose to rejoice.

There has to be a way to shift our thinking back to God's ways. Very few things in our current secular world encourage this thinking. We have to know this thinking in order to correct our own tendency toward it. I have been so guilty of letting upset thoughts take me to places where I was never intended to spend countless hours. It's very easy for our thinking to get off track from the earliest part of any given day and spend the rest of the day taking that undesirable path.

When our first thoughts are intentional ones, our following thoughts have a greater chance of being right and good. We really do have a choice in where we spend our days mentally. We make more choices each day than I think we realize. It is up to us to see things from God's perspective and in order to accomplish that, we have to reset our thinking throughout the day intentionally.

I am grateful for a husband whom I can do this with. We love each other enough to point out to one another when our thinking has taken a path that needs to end. I have also been blessed with some wonderful friends who will be lovingly honest with me when I question my own thinking and need perspective. We need others who can and will help us keep our hearts and minds fixed on a perspective of "rejoicing and being glad." The alternative is what? I'd say that it would be complaining and sadness, possibly anger.

It's so important that we take time out in our daily living to be reflective over how we are walking through the days we are given. Nothing tells us that we have lots of days ahead of us. We are all on God's timetable. Why not slow down with me and determine to choose to rejoice and be glad intentionally? I do know that on the days when the burdens come, and they will, I can then cast those cares on God because He cares for me. I can also choose to take God at His word and know that He wants me to set my mind on things that are above rather than here below, in this world.

We can practice living with this kind of intention in order to change our lives and the lives of those around us. I promise, people notice when we live in light of God's design. And don't we want them to see Christ in us? We will look different because we will be living differently. Choose to rejoice today and find gladness as your companion. Let the thoughts that get you stuck flee that you might replace them with rejoicings over how God has cared for you through all things.

Dear Father,

I come to You before this day begins asking that You would set my thinking in the right place. I know that there are things from yesterday that long to take up space in this day and I'm looking to You to help me focus instead on You and Your plans for me. Help me choose to rejoice throughout this day and be a glad-hearted woman, through Jesus.

Amen.

Colossians 3:13 Matthew 6:14 Colossians 3:2
1 Peter 5:7

Living in This Day
Psalm 118:24

1. Would you describe yourself as someone who lives out your days intentionally? If so, describe.

2. Do you feel the need to rush through life? Even feel yourself trying to win the race? Why do you think this might be true of you?

3. How can you rejoice in the mundane things of life?

4. What helps you keep your mind set on God's perspective?

5. How are your choices influencing the choices of others around you for good?

Surviving Sin

"And the world is passing away along with its desires, but whoever does the will of God abides forever."

1 John 2:17

Death is not a topic most of us choose as our top five picks on most given days. If you have experienced the death of someone dear to you, then you know that it isn't a comfortable place to dwell. It is the eventual outcome for us all in our physical bodies. On a spiritual level we know that death in this world is the beginning of our life in eternity with God.

In the verse above we are told that people are not the only things that are passing away. We are told that the world is passing away. Do you ever look around you at the examples of death that are the end of life? For example, I have a rose bed and I honestly look forward to summer for its blooming to reveal the new life of buds. Those buds will come, they will bloom and yield sweet aromas. But in a short time, those beauties are going to decay and die. If I don't tend those bushes year-round, then they will themselves die. They depend on me for their sustenance and tending.

The reason the world is passing away is due to the sin choice that goes all the way back to the first garden that God created. Within it He placed His creation of the first man and then the first woman, Adam and Eve. Everything was perfect, as was their Maker. But one choice, the only defined wrong choice, was made and sin entered the garden, bringing death and decay.

When decay and brokenness entered the world, it continued to multiply through people's choices that were not in line with what God had said to do. Disobedience brought destruction. If we look around us today, it's not hard to see how that sin has multiplied exponentially. One look at God's Word in the Bible will clarify that we as people are way off the mark of holiness. We live and deal with that brokenness and decay every day of our lives.

There are certainly times when the decay is more obvious to us and the brokenness personal. Rather than being overwhelmed by it, we can remind ourselves of why things are the way they are at present. The fall of sin began a long time ago and like a wheel rolling downhill, it has only picked up speed.

We were not created for sin and yet we live in sin as a result. Sin entered through a choice, one choice. There will be a day when sin will be no more but right now, we live on this side of eternity. In heaven there will be no more sin. So, while we are living in this world, how do we survive the sin that so easily entangles us? Here are five steps that

I have implemented into my daily walk with God in order to stand against the power of sin over me.

First, when I look at myself and my choices, I have to identify where sin and temptation are pressing on me. I then have to call it what it is, not make an excuse for how I might bend the Word of God to fit my desires. In acknowledging that it is sin I am identifying it and opening the door for a change in my position before God. Second, I choose to tell myself the truth, God's truth. I can only find that in the Bible. I have to do some homework on what I do know and seek to understand what God has to say about sin, my sin.

Third, I ask the Holy Spirit living in me, as a believer, to speak to me and show me what I need to see through God's Word to me. I need His help with the truth. Also, I must trust that when the Holy Spirit makes things clear to me, I am willing to act on them. What good is knowing the truth and doing nothing with it? It's just knowledge or fact. God sent the Holy Spirit at Pentecost to live within us and lead us as Christ in us, the hope of glory. When we trust the Spirit and hold God's truth in our hands, we are ready to pray with belief.

God has not given us a passive spirit but has given us power through the Holy Spirit. God knew that we would not, on our own strength and determination, be able to withstand sin and He sent Jesus to live and die for our sin. When we accept Jesus as our savior from sin and begin to live for Him, we are no longer our own; we are His. We may not have the courage at times to take the steps that we see ahead of us, but we have the confidence through Christ and with the Holy Spirit living in us to go boldly to God in prayer.

Fourth, we are told to pray believing that God can do what He has said He will do. We don't come timidly or apologetically but with a confidence that only comes through the Holy Spirit, our Encourager. This is where the hard part comes in perhaps. We have to wait patiently for God to answer our prayers. The scripture tells us over and over to wait on the Lord. In my experience this is the hardest.

However, if I have sought what God has to say in His Word, have been truthful with myself about my sin or temptation to sin, am listening for and trusting the Holy Spirit, and I pray believing, then my waiting will bring answer. Will it be the answer I want? Maybe. Maybe not. The purpose is to find what God wants for me, not what I desire. In the meantime, it is good for me to remind myself that God is busy, He is working. Just because we cannot see that work does not negate the work. That's where the truth and trust come into play.

Fifth, it is then our task to intentionally, with prepared determination, ready ourselves to endure whatever it takes. Like a long-distance runner, we must work daily at honing our skills through practice and skill development, in order to strengthen our resolve and ability to ward off the sin that so easily takes us down.

One thing I have learned is that the longer I walk with Christ the more I am challenged by Satan and sin. We become more knowledgeable and gain more wisdom and Satan raises the bar of his challenges to us. He never bothers the areas of our lives where we are practicing sin; he'd like for us to stay there and sin some more. He comes after those things in which he can do the most damage in our lives. This is all a part of the decay we talked about earlier. He loves to create chaos and doubt.

But thanks be to God! He has given us the way to have our sins removed through Christ. He has also given us His Word to take into our lives and use moment by moment. He's equipped us with the presence of the Holy Spirit, Christ in us. He is always with us and He's never going to leave us.

Praise God. Yes, the world is "passing away," but life in Christ is eternal and we have that hope set before us to strengthen us until we see Him face-to-face.

Dear Father,

You know our weakness just as You knew Adam and Eve's. You knew we'd never make it back from sin and the enemy of our souls apart from Christ's death on the cross to redeem us and take away that sin. Thank You, Father, for making a way for us to You before we even knew we had it. You are all-sufficient and good. Thank you, Almighty.

Amen.

Hebrews 4:16 Romans 5:21 2 Corinthians 5:21

Surviving Sin
1 John 2:17

1. If sin is a choice that we make, how do we avoid its temptations? Give examples.

2. Even trying to avoid sin, we will sin. How do you respond to your own sin?

3. Do you practice telling yourself God's truth in order to help you see when you are buying into a lie?

4. Is coming to God for forgiveness something to be ashamed of or thankful for?

5. What has God given us in the presence of the Holy Spirit to overcome sin? Is God working through your sin for your good?

Overwhelmed, Not Overcome

"Do not be overcome by evil, but overcome evil with good."

Romans 12:21

Is it just me, or does life just seem to get faster and more full with every new day? I don't think I've mastered the balance of the pace in my life at this point. I am prone to say yes to things and think about what is required later. Before I know it, I am in deep in a multitude of ways and directions. Sound familiar? I find that I can spend an entire day at home and end up just as overwhelmed as I'd have been if I'd left the house. I always see lots to be done.

At some point the pace wins every time. There are seasons of life that just tend to be more demanding than others for us all. But if we find ourselves constantly at the point of feeling overwhelmed, then we need to pause and ask ourselves what needs to go. Now, we can't get rid of our children, husbands, pets, etc. But we can certainly look at where our "extra" is being spent.

I come from a long line of individuals who just cannot be still, and I take that into consideration almost daily. It is my nature to go after life, not let it come to me. I can be pretty zealous and thrive on being engaged with others. However, I am a woman who desperately needs her still and quiet time. The pace has to drop off, or I become that other woman whom I don't even like.

So, how do you get to the place of being overwhelmed? Here are a few things that I have learned about myself. I must have sleep to be at my best. I need to start my day as slowly as possible. I need coffee before conversation and Jesus before my husband. Beyond that, I need to pace myself down, not up. It's important to know yourself before trying to figure out or diagnose someone else. For me, that takes a good bit of self-reflection and quiet.

Life has not always allowed this kind of time, and I've had to learn how to make it happen. When I was a young mother, I worked hard to get my day completed and my little ones in bed so that I could have some time to be an adult. In midlife, I used drive time to get alone and then grab moments in my day at work to be alone. As a schoolteacher there were not many of those. I also worked hard to get things done during the week so that the weekend would be for "other" more enjoyable things and time for sabbath rest and worship. At this stage, which is retirement, I have found it much easier to manage the best choices for myself and yet there are indeed times of being overwhelmed.

Some of this overwhelm is the result of life and some is due to my choices. When the circumstances of life overwhelm us, it is the most important time to prioritize what we need to continue. As we look at where we can cut things out, the last thing we should cut is our time with God. We need Him first. Let something else go, but if anything, increase your time with Him. He has taught me that it's okay if I fall asleep when trying to spend time with Him. He is here to catch me in all circumstances.

We need to remind ourselves that He understands our frame and He loves us right where we are, at every moment. He knows better than your husband, whom you tend to choose to lay all of your worries and woes before. Unfortunately, he cannot do better than God, and he can't see everything about your heart, no matter how much you want him to. I am guilty. Why emphasize the importance of God at times of craziness to the point of overwhelm? Because He is the way to overcome.

God does not desire for us to be overcome by life. He is a God of order, and He desires the best for you and me. We have to stay tied in tight to Him in order to stay the course away from being overwhelmed. On those days when you feel the seam of life unraveling, it may indeed be unraveling. Sometimes it is not. Going to God and telling

Him your heart and its needs will always open the door for change. He wants you to come to Him and let Him do the recalculating with you.

I have had what I would call some pretty severe times in my life and yet even in the most intense of all, I could cry out to Him. I recall one period of great challenge, when nothing came with any ease for quite a long time. My little prayer was, "God, just don't let me go." It was enough. He held on tight. In fact, He has never let me go. Others have, but my God, He has never failed me. He's never let me slip over the edge. When I feel the limits of myself and fear the edge growing near, I run to Him. I've learned that I don't have what I need, but He does. I run to Him. My husband gets the second call, but God gets the first.

As you begin this day or find yourself reflecting on it, ask God to show you how to follow Him more closely in the difficult times. Tell Him that you want His help in seeing how to do life more clearly in order to make your days count for more than constantly being overwhelmed. Also, ask Him to show you where you need some adjustments to your responses to more in order to choose less. Remind yourself that He promises never to leave us or forsake us. Then, go and do what He has given you to do as unto Him with a heart of thanksgiving. We want our lives to reflect Him to others, and He is never overwhelmed. He, instead, is always available. Run to Him and be saved, one day at a time.

Father,

Thank You for knowing our frame and our limitations. We certainly don't see them in obvious ways at times, Lord. Would You show us today how to see the boundaries You have safely set about us and help us stay within them for Your glory and our good? Thank you for never leaving us where we are. We come to You.

Amen.

Psalm 55:22 Colossians 3:23 John 10:9

Overwhelmed, Not Overcome

Romans 12:21

1. Do you find yourself feeling overwhelmed by daily life? How so?

2. What things tend to be the hardest to change when you are in the place of overwhelm?

3. What can you do differently in order to slow your life to a healthy balance?

4. How do you spend time with God each day? Does this time only occur when you need Him, or does it include wanting Him?

5. God can help you overcome in your daily life. How will you ask Him to do this for you? Give some examples.

To Be More Like You

"By this all people will know that you are my disciples, if you have love for one another."

John 13:35

Today, I ran into a friend whom I met over forty years ago. I recall the first time I met her. I had pursued her about carpooling to work in a county outside our immediate area. I was a new teacher in the area, and she had been there awhile. She had a little girl still in diapers at the time, and we were both young. I was so thankful to have her there to reach out to and ride with. We connected in the commute, and it mattered.

Our lives shifted a great deal over the span of forty-something years, and lots of changes occurred. We stayed connected, but very loosely. I had great respect for her as an educator, and she was a strong woman who knew what it meant to advocate for her students. We were both in special education and I learned a great deal from her during those two years we traveled together. I believe she made me a better teacher. She seemed to handle things with ease, and she was a woman of commitment.

I saw her down the road of time and learned that she had added a son. I had added three daughters. I was no longer in the classroom, but she was still fulltime. We would catch up quickly and share our life's journeys, as if no time had passed. I knew that her family was important to her and supporting them was her utmost priority. Our times together always left me with a feeling of having been "at home" with her.

The years traveled forward and after a season of being out of the classroom, I returned fulltime. We once again bumped into each other and caught up on the things that mattered. Let me just interject here how thankful I am that God kept bringing her through my life, time and again. He made sure I saw her and that our time was valuable. I recall praying for her and the things we would share at those catch-up times. I knew in a nutshell what the concerns of her heart were. I'd leave her but took the things she'd shared and prayed over them. Some things I did not stop praying for.

But then one day I ran into her, and I saw a different woman. The strong woman was present once again, but there was a lasting pain in her expression. We began to talk, and I heard brokenness, which supported what I had seen in her face. I felt concern in my heart immediately and asked how she was doing. I learned that a dark place in her life had ended in loss. How deeply I felt her grief, and yet I knew I could never truly know the depth of her personal grief journey. My heart ached for her because she was the one who always found a way to smile. The smile was dim and forced.

For a time, I questioned God, asking why He had not heard my prayers for this woman He had taught me to love. I did not understand, and I knew that she did not. None of us fully entertain where life's challenges might take us, and yet we arrive there. In those moments, we know how utterly dependent we are on God, and yet we feel so totally lost. I knew she was lost, and I wanted to pick her up and carry her for a while. I found it hard to walk away when we finished talking. I struggled for days but knew that her struggles were far greater, and it broke something inside of me.

One thing was certain: I spent a lot of time talking to God. As the questions and concerns arose, I turned them into prayer for her and her family. I wanted to pour something over them and somehow make it all better, but that was not for me. I had to seek the Almighty with every desire and call upon Him because He was near to both of us. I continued in prayer for her until I ran into her again.

Several more years passed, and I was back in her presence today. I saw the lady I met over forty-plus years ago. Her smile was there, her strength was there, her talk of her family was there along with talk of education and how she was still contributing to the lives of children. My heart was rejoicing! God does restore the days of our lives that are harsh and relentless through His mercy and grace. He does so in His own timing, however. Did He hear those prayers I prayed for her, for her family, her struggles? Yes, He heard every one, and He did what was best even though we may not understand in this lifetime.

Today when I left her presence, I was certain that God had kept my friend in His perfect peace because her mind is focused on Him. We will all walk through the valley of the shadow of death, and we will recall that God was with us if we choose to embrace His truth. My friend has done this and continues, not in her own strength but His. She can stand because He holds her up.

What a privilege it is to walk alongside others' lives in prayerful support and active love. Don't let your own life get you so bogged down that you forget to look to the needs of those around you. God desires our intercession for those He brings to us who need more of Him. We will possibly be in their place someday and welcome those prayers unknown. Pray without ceasing for the one to your side. God will hear and answer. I'm certain: stay confident in prayer.

Dear Father,

Thank You for how You order our days and bring things to pass that we neither anticipate nor expect. Thank You for the blessing of others in our lives that You designed to be there to make us who You want us to ultimately be. You are ever faithful, but Lord, sometimes we just can't see it, and I ask that You give us more faith today for that which we cannot see. Help us to trust You more each day.

Amen.

Isaiah 55:6 Isaiah 26:3 Philippians 2:4

To Be More Like You
John 13:35

1. Do others know that you are Christ's disciple by how you love them? What does that love look like?

2. Give an example of how you've put yourself aside to love someone else when God brought them to you specifically.

3. If God puts someone repeatedly in your life, do you ask Him what His purpose is for you both?

4. How do you grow your love for others in an ongoing way? What are some things you do?

5. In what way do you desire to become more like Christ?

Three Promises

"'For the mountains may depart and the hills be removed, but my steadfast love shall not depart from you, and my covenant of peace shall not be removed,' says the LORD, who has compassion on you."

Isaiah 54:10

In a world of instability and chaos, we are all seeking something that we can hang on to. Many are quick to give their word, yet following through with action often fails. We are indeed living in a time of broken-down communication. And yet communication is the key to functioning with one another in this world. Jesus tells us in the New Testament before His death that we, as believers, are to go and tell others of the gospel. How can we tell without communication?

We need to both hear and see that truth still exists and that we have not been forgotten. We will surely not find this truth if we look to the world around us. But God knew that this would be true, and He therefore gave us His holy Word. In that Word, found in Isaiah 54:10, He makes us aware of just how the circumstances around us can get rather desperate, and yet He has not moved. He has promised that He will remain the same for you and me.

I've found that I no longer welcome worldly news to guide my thinking. I don't find truth there, so it is best for me not to pursue it. However, I do read, and it doesn't take two seconds to find disaster upon disaster in the world. Whether it's storms of greater proportion and frequency than ever before, raging fires and floods destroying entire cities, children being killed at school by shooters, or wars that are destroying lives and the inability to build a life in one's home country, all are great disasters.

These are the realities that drive me to the verses that speak about God's grace on a regular basis, how we need God's grace to find hope and continue to seek out those who need salvation through Him. We who have Him have life. We have hope. We have love.

God loved us enough to tell us in Isaiah 54 that the world might experience great devastation. Therefore, we needn't be surprised by it. He gave us the heads-up that these things would potentially be occurring. More importantly than that devastation is what's found in the second part of that first sentence, "my steadfast love shall not depart from you." So, when we are tempted to embrace the devastation and fix our eyes on it rather than God, we need to remind ourselves and one another that God's love for us is unchanged and right here with us. It has not changed from the beginning of time. He generously reminds us that He loves us and that love won't be moved; it is steadfast. I love the definition of "steadfast." It means "resolutely or dutifully firm and unwavering."

So, the world may shake all around us, but God and His love will never be moved. I don't know about you, but I need that good news every day! Our God is not finite like the mountains, oceans, or people. He cannot be compared. His love is the real deal. When chaos arises in our world, as it often has, there is one thing that the enemy of our souls seeks to disrupt, first and foremost: our peace.

However, this verse goes on to assure us that God has taken care of that one, too. He reminds us that He has given us this truth, "my covenant of peace will not be removed from you." A covenant is defined as an agreement. This makes it a binding relationship through commitment. This will not be broken. No matter what is happening around you, you are assured that God has given you peace. That means it cannot be taken away. I think we have to be very careful not to forfeit that peace for a lesser worry or concern. God has this, why would we question it?

The final thing that this verse lets us know is that our God is a God of compassion. He has compassion for us in these sinful lives that we live. He sees our limits and has great compassion on us despite that sin. This verse indicates that the Lord Himself "says" this. Can we take Him at His word? I think the greater question is, will we take Him at His word? It is quite easy to lose our focus in seconds and find ourselves on the road filled with wrong thinking. Satan does love to disturb that covenantal peace that is ours from God.

We have to prepare for the moments that unsettle and shake us before they occur. We need God's words long before they need application. Those words have to be familiar enough for us to repeat them to ourselves when the lies begin to undermine our thinking. We need to do our homework with God's Word and know it for ourselves. How else can any of us endure the circumstances we face daily? We certainly don't have the power or energy to build ourselves up to the point of continuing.

However, we do have a God who has compassion for us and has assured us of His love for us, which will not be changed by anything. We have a God who has already given us peace through covenantal agreement; it's ours. We have only to receive it from Him. Hold fast to these truths as you walk through this day and tell yourself of God's truths that are unchanging. Put your name in these blanks: ___________, I love you steadfastly, ___________, you have my peace, ___________, I have compassion on you.

This is good news, my friend. Let it wash over you today and every day as you seek to walk in this world of sin. God has indeed made a way, even if we cannot see the way. He will reveal it to us when we seek Him. He is the Way.

Almighty God,

Indeed, the world grows darker with sin every day that we live in it. You are not surprised. You, who know all things, have gone before us, and in love, You have told us what we need to hear in order to continue. Thank You for Your Word and all that it gives us every day. It is life and breath, Lord. We trust in Your Word alone. Thank You for loving me, for giving me peace, and for having compassion on me today.

Amen.

1 John 5:12 1 John 4:10 John 14:27

Three Promises

Isaiah 54:10

1. Think of something in your life that fits the description of "steadfast." Describe.

2. What fears are you challenged by in today's world? Give examples.

3. If God has given us peace, then it is ours and cannot be taken away. How will you personally work to overcome your fears and replace them with peace?

4. How can you prepare for the challenge and temptation to fear? What will help you most in this process?

5. Place your name in the three promises and determine to tell yourself the truth throughout this day.

   _______________, I love you steadfastly.
   _______________, you have my peace.
   _______________, I have compassion on you.

I Run to You

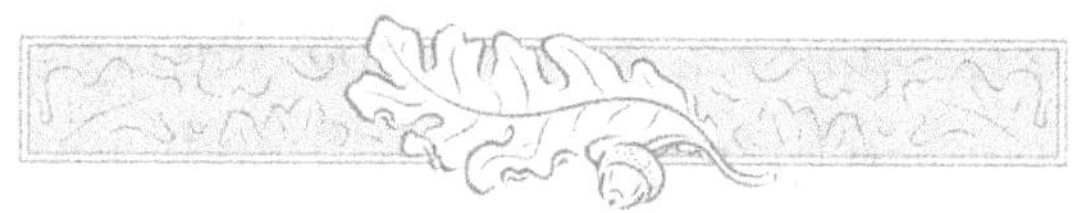

"Whom have I in heaven but you? And there is nothing on earth that I desire besides you. My flesh and my heart may fail, but God is the strength of my heart and my portion forever."

Psalm 73:25-26

I live my life surrounded with music because it brings me a sense of God's presence and joy. One group that I have enjoyed for years is Selah. Several of their songs stay close to my mind and heart. Today I started thinking about the song entitled, "I Look to You." The refrain says, "I look to You, I look to You, after all my strength is gone, in You I can be strong." Do you ever find yourself feeling the need for strength? There is good news, it is available through Christ. I'm so blessed to have good girlfriends and a great husband, but they can only offer my heart so much strength and help. Their love and support are everything to me as I walk through this world, but at some point, they're not enough. It's so easy to take the wrong road when we feel that our heart and flesh are failing. Perhaps like me, you've traveled a few of those roads and never want to choose them again. God knew that would be true of us and he gave us these verses through David in order that we might have the assurance that He understands.

The Psalms were definitely written for me. David is my guy in that he feels, he struggles, he falls down, he fights and gets back up. He was one determined warrior. And yet sin was always there tempting him to find that ramp off of God's road.

Ultimately, he always came back to God. David understood his need and dependency on the real and living God. He knew it best.

We are no different than this brother whose story is spelled out for us in writing. David grows to know himself well through the living out of his days. We are no different. We cannot know today what we have not lived tomorrow. We get there as he did, one day at a time. My father always used to say that phrase, "one day at a time." I used to get frustrated when he'd say it because I am a "go-getter girl," as I've related before. Dad was right though; we can only live in the day we are in.

It's really humbling when I see myself in my adult children. We feel pretty sure that through their growing up we have had an influence in their lives. Then one day we see them do something exactly as we would do. Sometimes I rejoice over those moments and other times I cringe. One of those celebratory times for me was when I went to visit one of my girls at work on her birthday. She happened to be running a meeting with her managers and she welcomed me to join them.

She continued with the business at hand, and I watched her lead this group of people with a confidence and maturity that just about brought me to tears. I'm so glad no one asked me anything because I probably wouldn't have been able to speak. She had taken the personality that she came into this world with and had developed it to the degree that watching what she was doing was beautiful. I marveled at how gifted she was at what she was doing. This was a moment of great rejoicing.

But there have also been moments that have come from the side of my wanting to cringe. No one wants to watch their child take on their sin behavior, and yet we do pass that on through our modeling also. It's in their display of our behavior that is undesirable that we want to disown ourselves.

This begins to show itself very early in their lives as they mimic our actions and choices. I recall being in the grocery store with them once, and everyone was out of sorts. I did not want to be there. One of them started asking me to buy ice cream before we entered the store. A sure sign that I was in for a battle. Well, she pressed on throughout the trip and by aisle eight she was building her case as to why we should be buying ice cream, even though I had made it clear that we would not be buying any.

She decided to pull out the big guns at that point and started telling me that we didn't have any ice cream because I had eaten the last of it. The truth was not that I had eaten ALL the ice cream, it was my weakness. I just didn't love how she was publicizing it to everyone else in the grocery store. It was a cringe moment and in the end we went home with no ice cream.

This is a minor example when compared to the whole of life's cringe moments. Like David I've had my times of weakness and rejoicing, both. If we look within we will find that we all are much like David. He faced some really tough consequences through his sin and at times sinned over and over again. But he never lost sight of whom he belonged to and needed the most. I've been there too.

Sometimes our sin can drain us to the point of physical and mental exhaustion. I like to refer to this as the time when "I run out of me." The only place I know to run to at that point is to God. Really, who else but God is there in the darkest moments of our sin? At those moments if we get real with ourselves, we, like David, will voice that God is our strength and our portion forever. Why does it take getting to that point? I don't know about you, but for me it's because I forget that God is God, and I am not.

In moments of great rejoicing, we quickly run to Him as if to say to Him, look, Father, isn't this amazing? Thank you. But when we're in those cringe moments of our sin choices the last thought is, wow, God, isn't that amazing? We know the shame of sin all too well at that time. That's when it's time to run to Him with a fresh need of forgiveness and delivery.

Sin can be a heavy weight at times, and I think God uses that weightiness to remind us to look at our feet and see what path we are on. Oftentimes we have lost our way yet again. But David reminds us that we can run to the Father, especially when our sin is all over us. God can handle that and in those moments with Him He understands exactly where we have been, when we switched paths, and He welcomes us back to the way that leads to life. That's usually when I realize that all I've ever needed is Him.

Beloved, we always need the Father. He is always waiting for us to look up and see that He has not moved, we have. He longs for us to come back to Him. Where else do we find this unconditional love apart from God? Run to Him in both the good times and the bad. He's not as far as you think He is, and He's not condemning you even half as much as you might be condemning yourself. He longs to forgive you and enfold you. As the song I referred to earlier says, "And when melodies are gone, In You I hear a song." Listen for the sound of His music and find that He is a God who keeps His words. The music is still playing and the melody sweet. Look to Him and sing His song today.

Father God,

You are all I need; forgive me for the times when I forget to come to You first. Your unconditional love has always met me no matter how I have come to You. Thank You, Father. Please keep teaching me to know You so intimately that I don't think, I just run to You. Oh, Lord, make me like David, a woman after Your own heart.

Amen.

2 Corinthians 12:9 1 John 2:1 Psalm 105:2

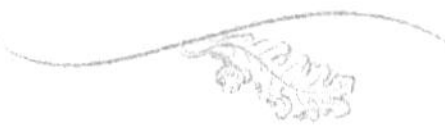

I Run to You
Psalm 73:25-26

1. In what way do you relate to David when reading these verses?

2. What moments of desperation have you had that derailed your efforts to follow hard after God?

3. How did God get you back to the path of His will? Describe.

4. Which do you feel more, God's conviction of your sin or your condemnation of self due to sin?

5. Write down three true thoughts of how God really feels about you that cause you to want to run to Him.

Focus, Focus, Focus

"Looking to Jesus, the founder and perfecter of our faith, who for the joy that was set before him endured the cross, despising the shame, and is seated at the right hand of the throne of God."

Hebrews 12:2

Many of us begin a new year with new goals. Sometimes those goals are redo's because we either didn't finish them, didn't meet them, or gave up somewhere along the way. Sound familiar? It does to me. Here in my sixth decade, I could probably generate a long list for you. Some of those goals might have been achieved and you set a new one just to keep yourself striving in the right direction in your life.

I recall when I was in my second year of college, I decided that I would start running daily. My parents had picked up running, and I thought it would be a good goal for me as well. It was a goal that I kept for several years, and I even ran some races with my folks. On the other hand, I have started one too many diets that either fizzled out, plateaued, or I simply gave up on. I have been a successful dieter and even kept the weight off for five years, along with serious exercise. But life and choices fell apart over time, and I started to indulge beyond my "good choices."

What have you begun and failed to complete? What influenced not finishing that goal? Whether it is a diet, reading the Bible in a year, regular get togethers with an accountability person, scheduled dates with your spouse, or daily devotional times, we have all set goals and failed to meet them. When this happens, it can open a whole can of worms for us. It's very easy to beat ourselves up over these things and forget that God knows our limitations and sinfulness. He knows that we will fail. He is forgiving, but we don't always struggle with Him. Sometimes, we struggle more with ourselves.

Think about a little child who is trying to learn how to share, but selfishness reigns in their heart daily. You, as that child's mother, might choose to try to tell and help that child to see that it is better to give than receive. You might make sure that they have something else that they desire and encourage to give that other thing up. But whatever you choose to do, you already know that it will have to be repeated over and over in order for the child's heart to learn to control their desires. We are no different, we're just more grown up.

So, how do we turn this ship in the right direction and accomplish that impossible goal? I believe we have to begin with our thinking. Satan loves to go for us between our ears every time. If he can get us off track in our thinking, then he will have a field day. What we allow into our minds and spend time dwelling on will often become what we do. As we think it, we become it. If I tell myself that

I really miss that chocolate thing and I allow it to stay on my mind, in time, it will win over my determination to make a better choice.

Sound familiar? To reach these goals, we will have to practice overcoming our obstacles. We have to take that mental assault and determine that we are more committed to the plan than we are to our desire to cave in. When we are weak, we have to tell ourselves the truth. Then, we have to follow with the resounding truth that God is strong. We might not have it, but He does. The easier choice will always be to give in, and it is the hardest one we will have to make. This is a good time to remind ourselves of how we felt the last time we gave up on a good goal.

Commitment takes courage, hard work, change, and determination. We don't always consider those when we are zealously picking a new goal. Our enthusiasm covers our interest in the details. The truth is that all change takes effort. When we slip and fall short on a given day, we have to get back up and go after it again. It's good to learn from those failures because they can drive our determination. I believe God uses them to give us a steadfastness in our commitment toward that goal.

There may be days of defeat, but we don't have to let those days of defeat define our futures. We are so worth the goals in life that lie before us. God uses them to grow us into being more like Himself. When we look at scripture, we discover that we have a very consistent God who does what He says He will do. Isn't that our goal as we seek to be more like Him? It's tough, girls, trust me. But it is in these choices that we get a sense of the sufferings Christ understands. We see the faithfulness and fortitude that only God can provide, and we can also find victory over our own weaknesses. Left to ourselves, we can accomplish nothing, but through Christ, all things are possible. God stands ready to help us in these challenges. In fact, I think He is our greatest cheerleader. If we want what is good for our children, how much more does He want for us?

Remind yourself with me today that "we are more than conquerors through Christ" (Romans 8:37). If our thinking begins here, then who knows, we may hit those goals that we desire to accomplish through Him who gives us strength.

Dear God,

We are weak, but You are strong. We sing it as little children and know it as grown women, but Father, it is hard to live it daily. I don't have what it takes to overcome, but all praise to You for giving Jesus to overcome for me. Let me follow in His footsteps today and follow Your will over my desires. Keep teaching me, God, I'm getting there. Amen.

Luke 6:38 Luke 11:13 Philippians 4:13

Focus, Focus, Focus
Hebrews 12:2

1. What have you begun and failed to complete recently? Describe.

2. What influenced you to stop the process, and how would you do it differently if given a second chance?

3. What helps you overcome the desire to give in to sin? Explain.

4. What will help drive your desire to have long-term commitment to the things that you begin?

5. Do you believe you can overcome your own weakness? Can you see your way to becoming a woman of commitment and determination? How will you accomplish this mindset?

Are You Comfortable?

"Tremble you women who are at ease,
shudder, you complacent ones."

Isaiah 32:11

What does comfortable look like to you? I see a fall morning, fuzzy slippers, a mug of hot pumpkin-spice coffee, and a good book. Or does it look like a day without any commitments that leaves you free to do whatever you choose? It might also look like a day on the beach with the sun making you weak and the waves rocking you to sleep as you read a captivating novel.

There are times for us to be potentially in every one of these places because God knows that we need to breathe, to step away and then return. He wants us to delight ourselves in His presence and all of His creation. These things are not bad. However, if they are all we ever desire, then the warning of the verse for us today is a good one. God tells us that there is a time for everything under the sun, and I believe Him. But we also have a greater purpose than just seeking our own comfort as we go through our lives.

Why do we have warnings in life? Whether it is a timer, an alarm, a blowing horn, or a note written in red, there are numerous ways to draw our attention to the immediate. That place in life that we live every day. That signal tells us that something is either happening, has happened, or is about to happen. The Bible is full of warnings.

I took some time to look at a variety as I prepared for this writing. Just look up the word complacent and see what you find.

The danger for us occurs when we begin to desire our comfort over calling. This signals several things that we need to look hard at. Are we experiencing something that we are avoiding dealing with? Are we trying to make ourselves feel better because someone has made us feel bad? Are we just tired of the world and going into it, so we stay at home hunkered down? Or do we just want to feel better?

God gives us times of rest and relief, and sometimes in beautiful ways. He knows the weight that we are under, and He has great compassion for us. He understands our need just to walk away from our daily grind to return to a much better place because we have let it all go. But after those times, He does have things for us to be about.

So, how do we get into those places of complacency that we may or may not be able to get out of? At times, we arrive there because we have failed to see and heed the warnings that are going off around us. It can definitely become a slippery slope very quickly. When we ignore the prompting of the Holy Spirit's warnings, we are getting deeper into a dangerous place.

The thing is that when we feel like we need to run or escape, our feet need to be on the right path. The path to God. It is definitely not the time to run from Him but to Him. Maybe you've taken some time off to get your head together and feel the pull to stay there. That's the time to find a sister who is a truth talker and open up with her. She can help you sort out your feelings and help you back to the path. It is not the time to call that friend who will complain with you and leave you deeper in the mud.

God tells us to seek Him, and we will find Him. So, seek Him and take those thoughts to Him. Tell Him that you can't or don't want to but tell Him where you are struggling. He gets it more than you know, AND He loves you. He will show you that He has a purpose in every day that He leads you into. Also, remind yourself that He has told us to "go" into the world, not run from it. He is busy doing His work in this world we live in, and how can we be involved if we do not move into it?

Remember, it isn't all about us. Yes, God is concerned for us, and greatly so. But He is also greatly concerned about using us for "good" in this broken world we live in. That means we must go and tell others what living in Christ has been like for us. He is far from done with you, so tell Him what's on your heart today. Ask Him to get you beyond yourself and your comfort zone. It is in those most uncomfortable places that He is often doing the greatest works. We will see that work if we endure and press on in Him alone. We will indeed see His hand accomplishing much. Keep trusting, keep being poured out for the many, and keep the light of Christ aflame in your heart through drawing closer to Him. He wants nothing more. And then, when the day is done and your household quiet, crawl up into His warm and loving arms and find rest for your soul in Him.

Oh, Father,

Give me a heart of purpose, whether at work or play. Sometimes, it is so easy to retreat and want to stay there. Teach me balance, o God. Thank You for times of quiet, delight, and rest. Thank You also for times when You call us to things that make us uncomfortable. You will be right there with us. Thank You that I will again find rest in the shadow of Your wings.

Amen.

Isaiah 55:6 1 Peter 5:7 Proverbs 3:5-6

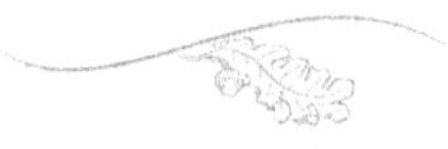

Are You Comfortable?

Isaiah 32:11

1. How would you describe comfortable from your thinking?

2. What is the difference between our comfort and our calling? Describe.

3. What are some warning signs that you recognize in your life?

4. Do you struggle with complacency? What is driving that desire? Explain in your own words.

5. Is there a way that God wants to use you that you are resisting? Have you told Him that you desire to follow Him with humility and obedience? Write your words out to God now.

What Makes You Proud?

"For our boast is this, the testimony of our conscience, that we behaved in the world with simplicity and godly sincerity, not by earthly wisdom but by the grace of God, and supremely so toward you."

2 Corinthians 1:12

When I think about the things in life that have made me proud, I realize that there are many of them. If you were to ask me, I'd probably tell you about my husband. First, I'd tell you how diligently he has worked to follow Christ and daily become more of God's man. Then I'd probably tell you about my daughters and the women that they have become and how their lives are impacting others for good. Then we'd have to grab a coffee because I would tell you about how wonderful my grandchildren are. One by one, detail by detail.

I could then tell you about the things I'm proud of in myself, either through my life or in my career. However, if I returned to considering this verse, I would have to get quiet and reflect to ask myself some good questions. When I look at the model of Paul in this verse, I'd have to look deeper to see whether I am living in the world with "simplicity and godly sincerity." I'd also have to consider if I'm relying on the wisdom of God for my testimony or on earthly wisdom. The things I am proud of might not be in God's design.

That is a bit sobering, and yet it is very helpful. We live in a time when women have fought and continue to fight to be recognized in the world so that they will be seen as equals. They work hard to make their mark on something that will have an impact for good and bring them recognition. They want to leave their mark on the world and improve it for other women. Inherently, there is no problem working hard at something you do well, but the reason for our doing it has to align with God's thinking. When I was working, I worked in a primarily female environment for a period of twenty-three years. Women can contend, trust me. We all seem to search for significance through our accomplishments. But how we do that matters, according to this verse. It's not that we shouldn't have an impact; it's a matter of how God desires us to accomplish it. Does our doing it bring glory to Him? We must consider who our efforts bring attention to in the process.

As I read this verse, I'd like to tell you about a precious woman who comes to mind. I met her when I was making my transition from being a special education teacher to a general education teacher. This was a big change because I'd never taught only from curriculums before that time. I had mostly developed curriculums for individuals and then implemented them. This lady was a woman who carried herself with an ease, and she intrigued me.

I saw her as an open door for me to walk through. She was beautiful both inside and out.

There were many times that I needed help, and I always felt I could ask her. She let me know that I was not a problem. She was that way with everyone. Her gentle spirit gave a comfort I hungered for. I could tell her I felt stupid, and she would let me know that we could do stupid together if need be. I found myself wondering, how did this woman get to be this way? Surely, she gets frustrated, impatient, exhausted, and over-extended, but she does not waver.

I used to love when she would tell me about her Saturday morning excursions. She had a practice of going to Dunkin' Donuts to get a coffee and two donuts by herself every Saturday morning. She was a lesson I needed to learn from. I continued asking her about her life to get to know her better. Her life spoke to me because she was so comfortable with herself. Through the journey, I began to understand how she became the woman I know and love today. Her road was anything but easy. God brought her a wonderful man later in her life who has faced death one too many times and has continually overcome it by God's grace.

He is a cancer survivor, a recurrent cancer survivor. To meet him is to love him! He's a crazy guy who plays the drums, tells it like it is, keeps everyone laughing, and fiercely loves his woman. Her love for him is always evident. This is only part of her journey. As I listened carefully to her words, I found a theme in her stories. She was a woman who continued trusting in God and took Him at His word. During times of awaiting test results or a further diagnosis of cancer, she prayed, voiced her faith in God, trusted God and demonstrated that faith in her continued daily demands. Her dependence was confident and singular. She walked through her days in simplicity and godly sincerity. Oh, how I long to be like her. She was a lot of things, but she was not consumed with the things of this world.

Being in her life directly for five-plus years definitely changed mine. I can't tell you that I know others like her. In my eyes, she is the picture of how NOT to get caught up in the world. I've done my best to recall and apply the things that she has embraced. Yet I realize that she has learned these things over time and through the challenges of life that she has faced.

The last little part of this verse speaks to the wisdom Paul and Timothy shared, as that which was by the grace of God. I also see my friend in this light. She seldom took credit for the things she did, and when she was recognized, there was sincere humility. She was always aware that it was not about her. How refreshing this sister in the Lord is to me still today. Just being in this world brings contention and competition along with way too much self-comparison to others. Overcoming this is a daily challenge for many of us. And yet, it is possible. I have watched it happen in my friend.

She has recently retired, but I am quite certain that she is not done going and sharing her wisdom with others. There is a world out there that needs more women like her and she's got to go share her testimony through daily living with others like me, who need her influence. Isn't it amazing how God works things into our lives in order to make us more like Him? How grateful I am for this one who continues to teach me how to live with simplicity and godly sincerity. I pray that my life reflects those qualities to others as a result of what she poured into me. May I honor her in my lifetime by doing the same. I pray her impact blesses your walk today, also.

Father,

Thank You for the women You have placed in our lives over the years to change us and conform us more to Your image. I thank You for this one who makes me smile by just a thought of her. She is so graceful, Lord, and such a picture of Christ to me. Teach me, Lord, to seek Your wisdom and not the wisdom of this world. Keep me from the temptation to chase the recognition of this world. You alone are what I need and desire.

Amen.

1 Corinthians 1:31 Psalm 34:2 Jeremiah 9:24

What Makes You Proud?

2 Corinthians 1:12

1. What things do you feel a sense of pride or accomplishment about in your life? Describe.

2. Do these things reflect simplicity and godly sincerity?

3. Can you say that your dependence on God is confident and singular? If so, give examples.

4. Do you struggle with comparing yourself with others or with their possessions?

5. How is your life reflecting a worthy example to others of Christ and His work through you?

Listen to the Wind

"And suddenly there came from heaven a sound like a mighty rushing wind, and it filled the entire house where they were sitting."

Acts 2:2

One of the places I love to be is in the mountains when fall is just about over. The hardier trees have not let go of their browning, dry leaves, and they hang on, waiting for their moment to let go. This is the setting that leads to one of my favorite sounds on earth. As the wind rushes down into the deeper areas of those mountains, the leaves begin to dance, and they make a most unusual sound. In my ears, it is a profound sound. It's not like any other sound I know. It can't be heard without the wind.

The sound they make creates a picture in my mind of them shivering in the cold. Apart from the wind, they make no sound at all. They just hang there, drying out until they fall to the forest floor. I've found myself standing in the freezing cold in an attempt to catch the sound of the leaves as they respond to the wind. If only I could find an adequate description for the haunting music they make.

I have also stood in the same location as wind gusts have literally come up with no notice to the point that it felt I might be lifted off the balcony. That's saying a lot because I'm no small thing. It may not have lifted me, but everything that could be moved on me was moved. I immediately thought of the rushing wind that appeared in Acts 2 at Pentecost.

Before Jesus's death on the cross He told His disciples that He would send another to comfort them in His absence, the Holy Spirit. It was at Pentecost that the Holy Spirit came and rested visibly on Christ's followers. There was a common sign amongst them all: a flame of fire above their heads. But a second occurrence took place at the same time. From heaven came a mighty rushing wind that filled the entire house where they were sitting.

Think with me about what that house had to have looked like after that wind occurred. If the rushing wind I experienced on that balcony felt as if it would lift me, then things had to have been moved in that place of meeting. Wind changes things, it repositions things, it creates movement, it influences all things in its path. Just ask anyone who has been in a hurricane, and they will tell you about the power of the wind. Or ask someone who has lived through a tornado, and they will express to you that the sound of the wind is powerful, like that of a locomotive train. It is a profound sound.

The wind of the Holy Spirit was no different on that day of Pentecost. It brought powerful change, and men spoke in languages that they did not know yet other hearers understood. The languages were those of men from their regions. They heard the result of the rushing wind at work in the lives of Jesus's followers. Later in Acts 2, the people who heard their own language spoken asked, "Brothers, what shall we do?" Peter responded, "Repent and be baptized every one of you in the name of Jesus Christ for the forgiveness of your sins, and you will receive the gift of the Holy Spirit. For the promise is for you and for your children and for all who are far off, everyone whom the Lord our God calls to himself" (Acts 2:38-39).

I think of this as similar to the wind and wind chimes. Depending on the strength of the gust, the chimes may involve only two tones. But a rushing wind causes all the pieces to ring out in a cacophony of sound. It's like a good symphony with a hundred instruments all sounding in one accord. The sound is full and bold. I think the day of Pentecost was one of fullness and boldness.

The wind brought the experience to life and made it tangible for those in limited earthly bodies. God made His presence known through the flame and the wind. Let me slip back here to my earlier story about being on the mountain and the sound made by the dry leaves and that experience of the rushing of wind. The sound of the wind, when those leaves were dry, was what captured all of my attention. The sound didn't occur without the wind. When the wind came rushing up and swirling as in a bowl, I felt the wind. But did I hear the wind or experience the result of the wind?

I have lived through a hurricane and a tornado, and by the grace of God, I arrived safely on the other side of both. The wind is powerful, and no, you don't always hear it. A meteorologist might argue with me on this point, but we'd miss the point. Wind has a very distinct effect on all things and I believe God chose to use the wind at Pentecost because it was His way of making them aware of His presence. The wind was like God, mighty. God knew that wind was something that these human beings could feel and had respect for because, like water, it cannot be controlled by man, only God.

God used what only He could use to make His presence known in the form of the Holy Spirit. We did not live in that experience of Pentecost, but we do live on the other side of it and, like the people who witnessed the speaking by men in languages that they understood, though the speakers did not, we have to ask ourselves, "What shall we do?" We know of the life of Christ, and we know He made it clear that He would send another to be the Comforter for us and that He would come to dwell in us through the power of the Holy Spirit.

You and I have been offered the opportunity to come to Christ and receive the Holy Spirit, Christ in us. Have you heard the wind, that nudging of heart that stirs you to follow God's lead? Do you recognize its unique sound, the still, small voice of God calling to you from within? The God of eternity longs to come afresh into your life and flow through you so that others might also see and hear Him. If God is stirring your heart over why you haven't made Him Lord of your life, please don't let these thoughts linger for you. The Holy Spirit wind is still blowing, and you are being offered the life that will create movement, repositioning, and change. God longs for you to repent and accept Him as your Father and Lord. He's ready to work in your life and create something beautiful. Can you hear the wind? Let it make you dance today.

Dear God,

Thank You for the stirring in my own heart long before I came to You. That stirring made me know just how much I needed You in order to be whole. Thank You for Pentecost and for making the evidence of the Holy Spirit indwelling tangible for us. Though You are limitless, You love us in our limited beings. You are not complicated, Lord. Thank You for the wind.

Amen.

Psalm 19:1 Colossians 1:16 John 20:22

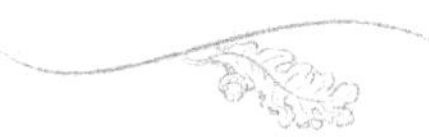

Listen to the Wind
Acts 2:2

1. How did Jesus send the Comforter to His people after His death?

2. If you are a believer in Jesus and have surrendered your life to Him, does the Holy Spirit live in you?

3. The wind and fire brought change to believers' lives at Pentecost. How has this same wind and fire changed you since you received Christ?

4. How do you experience the Holy Spirit living in you? Describe the ways.

5. What is a "wind" in your life that you are currently experiencing? Is it an easy change that God wants to bring, or do you find it difficult?

Ready to Respond, Not React

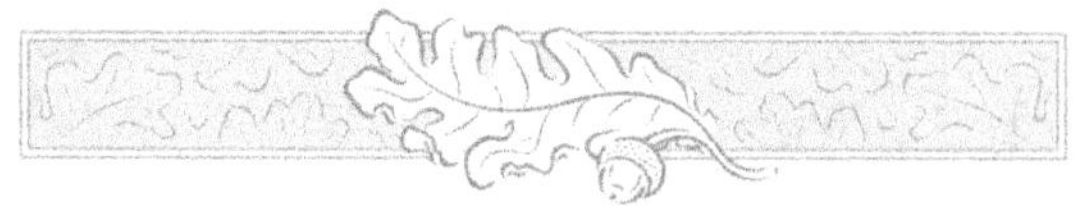

"Know this, my beloved brothers: let every person be quick to hear, slow to speak, slow to anger."

James 1:19

Think with me for a moment about things that we get "ready" for. We get ready for happy occasions, events, the day ahead of us, and lots of things. This morning, for example, I had a ministry event, and I made sure in advance that I was prepared with my talk, practiced it, and picked out clothing and accessories. I made sure that the food that I was to bring would be ready in time and would not delay me being on time. I checked in with my co-leaders and made sure things were on point. I was ready to address the day ahead of me before I got there.

Those times are easy to prepare for, even though we might face some battles in the process. However, there are also times that pop up that surprise us, and our reactions can be unready. In those moments, we have to make a quick choice as to how we will react to that unexpected thing. So, my question for us is, how do we prepare for those events that we don't foresee and assure ourselves that we can respond rather than react?

If I were able to choose life circumstances, I would definitely choose to have a prepared route. But what do I do when the unprepared comes? I find the answer is the same to both types of incidents. We have to be prepared for the unexpected.

No, I don't mean practical things here. We need to prepare spiritually, in advance, so that when the unexpected comes, and it will, we are able to respond like Jesus rather than Cruella de Vil.

This verse in James offers us the way to walk through the unexpected times. If we are prepared ahead of time with God's words, then we are able to stand in any circumstance. I actually love this verse because it's not my nature. I would get angry and start talking if I followed my own tendencies. But God says the first thing I need to do is listen. May I just say it is very hard for me to listen when someone is yelling at me. Been there, done that, don't like it. After being in that position several times, I began to see that the one unloading on me usually isn't as upset with me as they appear. For whatever reason, they have chosen to dump all of their trash at my feet rather than just the bit that we need to address.

I believe that it is crucial to gain understanding about anger. It is an emotion that, when out of control, can do so much damage, and the damage can remain for a lifetime. We have to be able to hear that anger and understand that its root is far deeper than it appears. Have you ever verbally taken someone to task over something and realized when it was over that you didn't feel any better? In fact, you felt worse.

That one coming at you has other things going on that have contributed to that place they are in. The scripture tells us that a soft word turns away wrath. That means I have been given the model to listen first and discern what the person is really addressing with their words. Then, as I speak, I need to do so slowly and gently. Oh, sister, this is a challenge for me. I don't know about you, but I grew up in a yelling household, and it's a habit that is hard to break.

With God's help, though, it is possible. Notice that the last thing to come into play is anger. Interesting, isn't it? Anger should be our last effort. So many times, things become a contention when anger is involved. But our point is to become a good responder to the unexpected incidents of life. Anyone can react, but usually that only incites. In time, that will go nowhere. Things can get stuck at that point and stay way too long, maybe forever.

I will say that there have been times that I have given a gentle word, and that only seemed to ignite the other person. I find that to be a true sign that the problem runs much deeper than us. If we are aware in advance that the anger may have a different source, we will more easily be able to listen well and, in turn, be more reflective in what we then say. A response isn't always necessary. Let me repeat that: a response isn't always necessary. In some situations, time must be given for the anger to boil down and a real conversation to be had.

There will be times when we should be angry. Jesus was not a passive Savior. There are times when anger is the appropriate response. The scriptures tell us that God has righteous anger. But we have to know a great deal about anger before we can use it appropriately. This is my thinking, anyway. Our time is well spent in knowing God's Word to us and how we are to deal with these issues long before they occur. That can only happen through knowing His Word. It means we have to spend time in the Bible.

God has given us the way to work on these things, and it is up to us to know what He has said. You won't find it outside of the Bible. The best time to prepare for the unexpected is before it occurs. And when it happens, think about what you know to be true. Stand on it, but do it through listening first, speaking when you are clear as to what will help in the situation to resolve the problem, and only think in terms of anger when it's clear that it is the right thing to do. Remember, it's the last step.

We as believers want to be equipped with what God tells us so that in our responses, rather than reactions, we will be like Him. Jesus's example went against man's first thought. He was long-suffering, patient, kind, and just. He was not passive. He was discerning, and He wants that for us, also. Through knowing of Him, we can equip ourselves to be like Him and bring peace where there is chaos. We have only to choose to respond to things rather than react. Our temptation will often be to react first and think later. But the outcome is not worth the damage that may never be healed. Make the choice before the situation occurs to respond out of the truth and the example that Christ lived out for us. We have been gifted with God's guidance through His Word, and we have the assurance of His presence with us. Your responsive following is possible through Him.

Dear Father,

Thank You for teaching us better ways through Your Word. Help us to set the discipline before us that will keep us in Your Holy Word that we might learn of You and live in Your example. Thank You for giving us all that we need for this day and all of our days. Help us to seek You always.

Amen.

Proverbs 15:1 Daniel 9:16 Ephesians 4:12

Ready to Respond, Not React

James 1:19

1. How do you prepare for events that aren't foreseen but need to be responded to rather than reacted to?

2. Is your first response in a struggle to listen? If not, what is?

3. How do you feel after you've taken your frustration/anger out on someone else?

4. If you listen first, what kinds of insights might you gain? Give some examples.

5. How will you work to put listening first in your responses and anger last? How will you sandwich in between those some slow words?

Getting Established

*"And after you have suffered a little while,
the God of all grace, who has called
you to His eternal glory in Christ,
will himself restore, confirm, strengthen,
and establish you."*

1 Peter 5:10

When all of us start out on our own in our early adult years, we generally feel great excitement and equal fear. Writing that first check for a down payment for an apartment and the first month's rent is a sobering experience. I still remember doing this in Columbus, Georgia, as I began my first full-time teaching job. I knew that there would be challenges, but going through them seemed worth it if it meant I would become established in my adult life. There were lots of rites of passage that were attached to that process for me, and I am guessing for you too.

Looking back on that season in my life, I can easily say that it sure would have been easier if someone else had helped me or done it all for me. But the point was that it was my time. It was now up to me. The journey included some fears and worries, along with some real difficulties. However, I was motivated and determined to make it.

My determination has been tested more times than not. I am still facing a lot of firsts, and yet the lessons God taught me then are still applicable today. In those struggles, God was always working for a greater purpose than the immediate problem that I could see. I had to get past those times to see how much He changed and strengthened me through those challenges. At times the purpose was to grow me up, other times it was to give me greater knowledge in an area. Sometimes He was teaching me patience, long-suffering, or true joy. Not everything was hard, but God was using those hard times with great intentionality in my life.

The above verse from 1 Peter 5:10 has helped me immensely to see how God is sovereign and has all things under control in my life. First, it points out that God has called me. I didn't just arrive in this place. Rather, He has taken up my life which I gave back to Him so many years ago and is using these things for my good. He picked me for this very thing. Let that sink in. God never tells us that life will be a bed of roses. In fact, He shows us here that we will suffer for what he refers to as a "little while." I continue to seek to understand that God's timetable and definition of time does not look like my concept of time. We don't know what that "little while" will look like when we are in a challenge. Often it takes getting on the other side of it to see clearly. There are also times when that challenge doesn't leave us but remains.

God does tell us next that He will "restore us." Let's look at the word restore. It means to bring back to a right practice, to return something to a former condition, to repair or renovate so that something is returned to a former state. I like the idea of God renovating my life. It is always very hard work that is time-consuming. It is physical and emotional and there is no rushing the job. But when the work is done, the delight over the outcome is great.

So, here's my translation of these thoughts. God is our contractor, if we have surrendered our lives to Him. He determines the work that can be done and the first job is demolition. Don't you just love those? And every woman shouted, NO! Life at that point is mess upon mess; anyone relating here? Then the verse goes on to tell us that He Himself will make us strong. God's work is for the "weak" despite what the world around you tells you. For when we are weak, then He is strong. You see, He loves us enough to tear away the things that need to go, even if it is painful. We might be a hot mess for some time as a result. We may have to wait for the new thing to be installed, and when we think we are done, we may not be finished.

I don't know about you, but many times I have stood in the open air and announced to God that my shoulders are not as wide as He thinks they are.

It's a good thing He doesn't listen to my rants and stop the process. However, I like to look for a way to retreat when I hear Him shouting "Onward!"

The final thing that God says about our suffering is that it will bring us steadfastness. What does that really look like? This will perhaps set you back, it did me. The definition says it is the quality of being resolutely or dutifully firm and unwavering. Well, then, I'd say that God has great plans for those of us he has called to Himself, and He is in the business of transforming us. He is doing that through our sufferings. He is with us, restoring us, strengthening us, and making us steadfast. No wonder it feels so tough.

Eternity is ahead of us and the path of this life will bring the very things we'd rather not have to face. However, knowing that God is doing a work in me sure helps me stay the course. It causes me to "continue" despite the struggle of my heart. We need not see our weakness as a failure within us, nor a punishment from God. It is part of His perfect plan for us.

If we choose to take what He has said to us in these words, then we know He is actively making us into His likeness. Don't resist when you see that challenge coming. Instead, remind yourself that God has chosen you and He always completes what He starts. Then walk in the light of His truth all the way. We will get there together.

Dear Father,

Give me a heart that is undivided when it comes to the changes You are making in me. Though it feels hard, even impossible at times, keep my eyes set on You. I want what You have for me and I trust in Your strength alone, for it never fails. Establish my ways according to Your perfect plans, I ask.

Amen.

2 Corinthians 12:9 2 Corinthians 9:8 James 1:3

Getting Established
1 Peter 5:10

1. Do you see your life as exactly in the place God has for it to be? Describe.

2. Is God renovating some area in your life presently? Give a few details.

3. Can you see the process of heart renovations as God's gift to you? Do you see His love for you in it? Explain.

4. How has God brought steadfastness into your life through struggles? How has it changed your responses?

5. How can you use these truths to strengthen someone else today?

The Family Picture

"For just as the body is one and has many members, and all the members of the body, though many, are one body, so it is with Christ."

1 Corinthians 12:12

We have been entertaining the idea of adding to our family. We are thinking about getting a second dog. Our dog is in his latter years and we've wrestled with whether or not we want to do the "dog life" in the future. The child-rearing years are behind us, and we have made a family with our Yorkshire terrier, Baxter.

Considering adding to the family brings lots of questions that are unanswerable beforehand. We will definitely be taking some risks and accepting a long-term responsibility in adding to the family. Life is full of changes and some of them we can choose, while others don't come with a choice. In this situation we do have a choice. I hope we make the right one.

Families are similar in a way. We are born into a family. We do not choose our parents, siblings, grandparents, or relatives. They are given to us through the process of what we know as life. The Bible has much to say about families through examples of families from the beginning to its ending. The first family is established in the very first book of the Bible, which is Genesis. It consisted of Adam and Eve. We all have a family of origin even if we are not raised by that family.

In the New Testament Jesus gives us the picture of what family is in a tender way, just before His crucifixion. He told His mother Mary, and John, whom he loved, "Woman, behold your son!" "Son (John), behold your mother." Jesus's direction to them was to be family to one another though Mary was not John's mother. Then in the verse for today we are given Jesus's teaching that we are all individuals and yet through Him we make up the body of Christ. A body functions as a whole and can't function fully without all members.

So, where am I headed with this? I want to take you back to my early childhood when I became acutely aware that God was putting individuals around me that were "like" family to me. I can't tell you that my early years were rich in truth and nurture, but I can tell you that God placed what I refer to as "significant others" around me at all stages of my development. One of the earliest memories that I have of the "family of God" came through a couple named the Edgners. They were a constant in my childhood. I was fairly sure that they were always at the church, though I knew they couldn't live there.

They took a real liking to me and treated me with so much love, respect, and affection. I honestly don't know what their specific role was in the church, but they were always in the kitchen cooking for events. I think they also were members of the church. I would find my way into that kitchen and they would sit me up on a stool, or give me an apron, and get me busy. Every memory of them is good. I eagerly looked forward to seeing them and being near them. In time, they gave me a name. Mr. Edgner's name was "Lou" and he affectionately called his wife "Shug." Together they chose to call me "Pie Dough." Why am I telling you this story? Because God knew that my heart needed loving and encouragement with focused attention that would help me see myself as He saw me. They helped me see Jesus and myself in a true light.

If I continued this road with you, I would have to list many names to fill in the spaces of those significant others that I looked to and learned from. At the time I had not seen that their purpose was to bring Jesus close for me. I'd grown up singing songs like "Beloved, Let Us Love One Another," but I didn't fully grasp what I was singing about until much later. This couple began a walk with Jesus and me in that kitchen and I experienced the love of God in them. It mattered then, it matters still.

Today being connected to the family of God is as essential to me as breathing air. God never intended for us to function in isolation but gave us a whole body to function with. It was designed by God. Families can get sticky sometimes and God knew that. Thus, He has a grander plan. Being connected with the body of believers on a regular basis is how we are able to continue life. They are my family, and their gifts differ from mine. We need one other. We grow together as we go through the ups and downs of life alongside one another.

God tells us not to give up spending time with each other, valuable time. We are given much instruction in the New Testament about our connection with the body of Christ. It is for us to seek out these things in order to understand how God has chosen for us to do life together. Nothing else can define what that looks like but the Word of God.

When we live according to the plan that God has established for us, we will find that we have all that we need. That means we have to meet, we have to engage, and we have to be vulnerable with one another. In order to really love, as Jesus did, we have to get our hands dirty. We must offer transparency with those whom He has deemed worthy of such a position. Not all will be worthy, and discernment will teach us that. Jesus left us the Holy Spirit, Christ in us, to aid in knowing what is true and what is false. He is here to guide us in these steps.

So, whether you grew up in a good and godly family, or you grew up in the worst of circumstances, take a moment today and look for the "significant others" that God has put on your path. Those individuals were put there by God to help you find your way to Him and complete this journey we refer to as life. I will always be grateful for the Edgners and all of the individuals whom God continues to put on my path who point me to Him. Don't ever think that you are in this alone. If you are a Jesus girl, you have an entire family surrounding you. Your family picture is larger than it may seem.

Dear Father,

It is so easy to think that we are alone in this life. The Enemy loves to deceive us into believing that we are all alone and no one would understand us or want to. Thank You, God, that this is not true. Thank You for the body of believers that You give us to live with and through our days. Being with Your family is my happy place.

Amen.

John 19:26-27 Ephesians 4:12 1 Thessalonians 5:11

The Family Picture
1 Corinthians 12:12

1. Do you have any "significant others" whom God has placed in your life?

2. How did you use them to grow in Christ? Give examples.

3. Are you connected to other believers through active fellowship? If so, how?

4. How are you investing in relationships with other women in order to develop transparency and accountability?

5. What are some ways to develop a stronger life with the body of Christ around you? How will you activate your ideas?

Choosing Right, Despite the Wrong

"Finally, brothers, whatever is true, whatever is honorable, whatever is just, whatever is pure, whatever is lovely, whatever is commendable, if there is any excellence, if there is anything worthy of praise, think about these things."

Philippians 4:8

If I asked you what you believed is the single most damaging thing in your thinking, what would you say? Would you say hate, envy, pride, greed? Those all carry a great deal of damage in and of themselves. My answer to that question would be one word: comparison. Think for just a minute about the things that trigger when we compare ourselves to others. One might say I become a better person by comparing myself to others. It helps me push past them and achieve greater things.

I do believe that we can look at others' abilities and achievements and grow from them. Others often inspire us to do great things. However, when we are looking at the person we are created to be, we have only one comparison to make, and that is to Jesus. We were created in His likeness and to reflect the same.

Satan loves to undermine our thinking through comparison. I am convinced it is one of his greatest tools. He seeks to block all that is right in order to get us focused on all that is wrong. He does so in order to create an ungrateful heart in us all. Comparison tends to make us forget our strengths and focus on our weaknesses. It can also leave us feeling defeated when there was never a competition. It can cause me to forget my God-given strength in order to concentrate on my personal weaknesses. It can cause me to want what I don't need until it consumes me.

God has told us to set our minds on things above. Comparison calls us to fix our minds on what is here and now, which is fleeting. And just like that, we are on a path that leads to destruction and despair. I have been in this place often, and it is hard to get out of once you buy into its power over you. Satan is referred to in scripture as the "father of lies." When he goes after our thinking through comparison, we are set up to find failure. Losing sight of the truth comes very easily, and we can end up knee-deep in anxiety and despair before we know it.

Have you ever gone into your refrigerator to get something out, and you get a whiff of something that is not good? You search around to see if a lid is open or if an obvious thing might be going bad, but you can't pinpoint it. You roll on with what you are doing, and upon returning to said refrigerator, you find that the smell has multiplied. This goes on for a few days, but you don't find the "obvious" item causing the stink. Then, one day, you have all you can take, and you start pulling out drawers in search of the culprit. Lo and behold, you find a portion of an onion that somehow got pushed to the back and over the top of the bin until it landed behind the drawer. There is what has been fermenting into the unbearable odor that has overtaken everything in your fridge. It's horrible!

We are the same way. We get a comparing thought in our minds; the damage begins to multiply. In time, we become stinky. We spread our fumes to others and even get frustrated with ourselves, and yet we don't look hard for the stinky thing. We may look passively but we don't search for the item going bad in us. As a result, we have a fully fermented mess on our hands.

What would have happened if we had searched diligently for the stinky item when we first smelled it? If we had continued until we found it and dealt with it? This is what God is calling us to do with thoughts Satan brings to our thinking through comparison. The only way to battle this wrong thinking is to replace the lies with the truths God gives us in His Word. He has never said to any one of us, I wish you were more like she is. Why do we ever allow ourselves to slip into these places of thinking? We do so because the deception is strong, and we live in a fallen world.

We have to keep our minds fixed on the truth above all else. The lies come so easily, and yet we have to see them coming and refuse them. We then have to replace those lies with the truth. It takes effort, and yet I can't think of anything that is more worth my efforts every day. Being a woman is tough enough without the stumbling stone of comparison. Trust me, I have battled this my entire life. I was taught to believe that I was less than God's best and found that when others weren't telling me that, I did a good job of telling that to myself. Comparison became my battle very early on in life. It took me years to know and understand what "truth" was in my life. But God got me there, and together we unpacked the lies stacked against me so that I could then embrace His truth about me.

Like most things in my walk with Christ, this has taken and continues to take practice every day. But I'm happy to say that at this point, when I'm being tempted to make a comparison of myself, I am quick to see a large red warning sign going off in my head. I then get busy replacing any lies with my God's truth. Thank God we have the Truth. I don't want to know where I would be without it. Choose today to start and end it focused on the woman God sees you to be. When temptations arise, as they will, choose truth and enjoy being God's girl.

Dear Lord,

Comparison is such a destructive tool in the hands of my Enemy. Thank you for knowing this would be the case and for giving me a way around his cunning lies. You alone are the reflection that I need and the goal I seek. Help me this one day to fix my eyes on you and come to its close with your truth ruling in my heart and mind.

Amen.

Colossians 3:2 James 4:7 Philippians 4:9

Choosing Right, Despite the Wrong
Philippians 4:8

1. What do you think is the most damaging thing in your thinking? Explain.

2. Do you struggle with comparisons in your daily life? Give some examples.

3. What are some things about you that reflect truth, honor, justness, purity, loveliness, commendableness, excellence, or are worthy of praise?

4. Do you search within yourself to see the ways in which comparison creeps into your thinking?

5. How will you apply trust in your life today from what you know to be true? What encouragement might you find?

When God Calls You

*"But Moses said to the Lord,
'Oh, my Lord, I am not eloquent,
either in the past or since you have
spoken to your servant, but I am
slow of speech and of tongues.'*

Exodus 4:10

In the Old Testament, there are many incidents where God speaks directly to His people, Israel. This was before Jesus was born, lived, and died. The Holy Spirit had not come to live in believers at this time. One of my favorite characters from that period is Moses. He champions my feelings of inadequacies when he speaks the above words back to God. Been there and done that. This happens to me every time I am asked to speak to a group of people. I'm always sure that someone else could do it better. But I also am sure at those times that God is calling me to do this seemingly impossible thing.

Moses, in this verse, knows exactly what God has told him to do, and he begins to negotiate with God by reminding him just how inadequate he is. This gets me thinking about my husband and I when we are considering making a big purchase. We collect the facts, research the product, list pros and cons, and look at customer satisfaction reports, as well as reviews. We cover all of the options that we can think of. We spend days with the information, and then the time comes to make a choice. Nothing happens until we act on that information. We have all that we need to make a decision, but we have to begin the process. Moses had everything that he needed, yet he questioned himself.

We can have all the information we need and still second-guess ourselves. Why is that? Do we fear the consequences of the choice turning out poorly or the reflection that it will cast on us? Do we question the financial loss that will be ours if this is not a good investment of our monies? This is good thinking, and yet, in this situation, God was the one advising Moses directly, and he was still backtracking. My husband and I would bring all of our findings to God and wait for Him to answer before we acted on it. We would give God time to throw the door wide open or slam it closed.

Moses was being told directly what he was to do, and he offered God all of the reasons he could not be the best choice to do these things. We are not that different from Moses. Can't we come up with some great excuses when we know that God is calling us to do something? I know I can. But think about God standing in front of you and telling you what to do, and you still have doubts.

I think you know what I am referring to. It's like when you receive an email that tells you there is a family in the church that is needing meals due to a hardship in their lives and God pricks your heart. You look at the dates and don't think any of them will work out for you. You scroll on to other emails only to find God calling your mind back to the need before you. And when you sign up for that meal and provide to minister to that family, God shows you why he pricked your heart. In those moments, we know that God was telling us what to do from the beginning.

The point is that God does not speak audibly to us today, but He does make Himself clear to those of us who are His people. The struggle comes, I believe, when we look at our flesh rather than God's unlimited power. Like Moses, we have callings, and God assures us that if He calls us, He will equip us. We have to respond to that call with faith that God will do what needs to be done. We are simply the vehicle that He chooses to use. The call on our hearts is to be willing to go and do as we are led.

God shows us through Moses just how far He goes with us to fulfill His calling. God kept making Moses face the call until he followed it. He had the right to skip over Moses and use someone else, but this was Moses's call. It was for him to respond this time, not seek out one who he thought would do a better job or relieve him of his. God loved

Moses to the extent that He continued to lead him to what he was to do.

God is the same today as He was back then. He has specific callings for each and every one of His children. We have to embrace those callings with faith that the One who calls us will indeed prepare us for the task completely. Our confidence and hope will only fully be found in Him.

So, what does God have before you that you are uncertain about? Have you taken it back to Him and asked Him to make clear what He is saying to you? In the times of great decisions and even in the small, I am learning to go to God and seek His will over these things that He puts before me. At times, I pray that He will make the answer so obvious that I will have no room for doubt in regard to His will for me. I am also learning to wait until He answers, even if I must say no, in order to be sure I am following His will. Sometimes, that means saying no, even though it is not the popular response.

If I really want to have the discernment of God's will, then I have to be willing to wait for it. And when He shows me what He has for me to do, I have to be willing to do it. My call is to take His direction to me and not continue to question whether I did the right thing or not. When I question after He has made it clear, I have to remind myself that I am questioning the God who created the entire universe. What does my doubt look like at that moment? This helps me get my perspective back where it belongs.

Lastly, I have to remind myself that God is not relying on me, I am relying on Him. I ask myself, has He been faithful in the past? Oh yes, He has been faithful to me. The question is, am I ready to be faithful to Him? Why does God take us through these things?

I believe the purpose is for our maturation in Him. He is still growing me up in discernment, and He'll use anything that is for my good to get me there. This process is known as sanctification. These are the ways of one who loves us and wants our best. So, you may feel like God is calling someone else other than you. But the truth is that He is lovingly calling you to this thing that is greater than you so that He can show you what He alone is capable of doing.

Dear Father,

You love us so well. You teach us with compassion and understanding. Thank You for overlooking our weakness of flesh in order to teach us of Your greater calling in this lifetime. In You, we find our hope and strength when the task appears greater than us. Keep growing us day by day until we reflect You to the self-seeking world around us. Be glorified in us today, Lord.

Amen.

Ephesians 5:10 2 Timothy 3:16 1 John 2:17

When God Calls You

Exodus 4:10

1. Do you ever struggle with self-doubt? Describe.

2. What is something God has called you to do that you've felt unequipped to do? How did that affect your choice to respond to His call?

3. What things in your thinking keep you from responding to God's calling?

4. How can you help yourself see God's calling as an opportunity for blessing? List some ways.

5. While you are waiting for God's discernment in what to do, are you waiting with a willing heart to receive His response?

The God of Possible

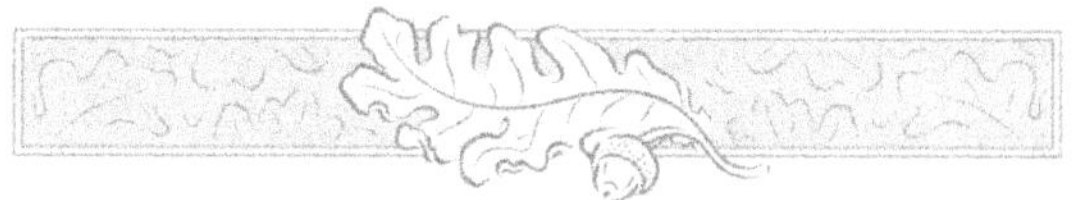

"For truly, I say to you, if you have faith like a grain of mustard seed, you will say to this mountain, 'Move from here to there,' and it will move, and nothing will be impossible for you."

Matthew 17:20

Think of a time when God has brought you to a place of decision over a new beginning. With it comes the vision of possibility and the fear of failing to complete the task. If we look at things in our strength, we will surely see our limits. But if we look beyond our ability and see God's capability, we are more likely to see great potential.

In the verse above, Jesus speaks to our faith and compares it to a mustard seed, something so tiny, and yet it yields something Repetitious when it is sown. Several years ago, God put a desire in my heart to begin a Sunday school class for special needs children at the church I was attending. I have a degree in special education and had experience over a good number of years so I was confident that I could accomplish the task.

I tried to put this idea on the back burner a few times as I considered what it would be like to commit to serving every Sunday and what it would cost me in sacrifice. God did as He usually does when He is calling us to do something. He kept bringing this idea to mind and parking it before me. But He added another component to it over time. He made me acutely aware of the parents who could not worship together, ever, because of the responsibility of their special child.

As you can imagine, God got right in my face and stayed there until I moved on this calling. I knew what He wanted to do through me, and yet I had to trust Him for the outcome. I wrestled with the choice that I was to make. Would I trust Him, or would I retreat? I moved forward and began with three children in a short period of time. God then provided some help, and for the first time in a very long time, these parents got to worship together.

I learned a great deal about myself through the experience of God calling me to serve Him in this way. One of the greatest lessons was for me to see His possibilities instead of my own potential failings. What I needed was faith of a mustard seed rather than fear of my own failure.

Over the weeks that followed, I watched as the Lord provided for the time the children and I were given to share. I was humbled by what I saw God do despite me. All I had to do was follow His calling of me, take the little faith that I did have, and sow it in the ground of my church. From it, God provided abundantly.

God wasn't asking me to see what the outcome of this calling would be. He was not asking me to get it all done perfectly. He was not going to judge me on my performance. He was saying to me, I have placed a need before you, I have equipped you with the skills needed, and I need you to do this. I had to only trust and believe through faith in His ability to accomplish it.

Why is it so difficult to have faith at times? We can grow ourselves a garden full of weeds of worry when we have been given a mustard seed's worth of faith that will flourish under the hand of God. I am currently in a situation that I am rapidly losing faith in, and I find it hard to produce much other than worry and despair. This obstacle continues to grow into a giant-sized opponent. Day upon day, it seems to multiply and further weigh down my heart. At times, I don't think that the tiny bit of faith that remains is worth sowing into the ground of my heart. I'm ashamed to say that it seems too little to focus on or make an effort toward.

This is how I know that I must get out my shovel and gloves in order to plant my faith once again in the fertile soil of God's garden. I know that I do not have what it takes to cause anything good to come from this struggle. But more importantly, I know that God is the Lord of my struggles, too. He is waiting for me to bring Him this burden, over and over if that is what it takes. He will cause the small belief that I have in Him to grow and multiply as a result of my placing my faith in Him alone.

I have cried out to Him over this situation, and I am confident that He has heard every one of my cries. I know that He has not overlooked my faith in Him. I have to tell myself the truth: He is still working this thing out for His glory. In the meantime, it is for me to place my hope and faith in Him and let Him turn my mourning into greater joy. When we feel the desire to settle for the impossibilities that are before our eyes, it is time to remind ourselves that God is the creator and that He sees all things. Then, we do well to take our eyes off our perspective and get focused on His.

We will go through some very difficult things in our lifetimes, and yes, we will want to give up and lay aside that mustard seed- sized faith that we have left. The Enemy of our souls will do all that he can to create despair and doubt in our hearts. At the same time, our God, the only wise God, is waiting for us to take that seed of faith and plant it deep in His fertile ground so that it might multiply into even greater faith.

Oh, Father in heaven,

There are times when it is so difficult to see our way in the things that You call us to. I know that You are keenly aware of all of these times. Father, would You keep our hands to the plow as we plant our faith in You? Give us hope where there is despair, and help us to see Your perspective over our own limited ones. If ever we needed You, Lord Jesus, it is now. Give us faith that will move that mountain.

Amen.

Luke 13:19 Luke 17:6 Hebrews 11:1

The God of Possible
Matthew 17:20

1. Do you ever find yourself resisting God's leading due to your own insecurities and fears? Explain.

2. Have you trusted God with a calling in your life that turned out as a life lesson rather than the blessing you thought it would be? If so, describe.

3. Why do you struggle with faith? Do you think all people struggle with faith?

4. What can you do to deepen your faith in God and minimize your worries? Write out your ideas and post them in a visible place for reference.

5. Describe someone you know who is the picture of one having "great faith." Let that person know that they are having an impact on you.

Blessed Assurances

"Behold, I am with you and will keep you wherever you go, and will bring you back to this land. For I will not leave you until I have done what I have promised you."

Genesis 28:15

Is there anything more beautiful than a sunrise or sunset? I am a sunset girl because I am a night owl who's married to an early bird. For me, sunset is that time when the chaos of the day quiets, and it feels as if God is saying, okay, this one is coming to a close. All of the crazies of the day are stilled, and we seek out how to tuck this one away.

I know that whether it's in seeing a sunset or a sunrise, I have an abundant sense of gratitude. All of nature reflects the glory of God, and in its characteristics, we see the peacefulness that is ours. It's easy to feel thanksgiving in those moments. All of this got me thinking about the many ways God blesses me through each and every day. His assurances are many and accompany me through both my days and nights.

When the day gets off to a rough start, I have the assurance of His words that tell me He is still with me. When the puppy pulls the moss out of the potted plant for the fiftieth time that day, I can remind myself that God gave this animal to me for a purpose and that she is a beautiful creation. When I put my lips to that steaming coffee that tastes like a burst of fall to my taste buds, I can thank God that I have what I desire and enjoy it to the fullest.

We have so many assurances from God to sustain us through the days. I hold tight to the assurance that God is with me and ever-present. Just knowing He is with me is a blessing and a reminder that He never sends me into anything on my own. He always has my hand. We also have the assurance that He loves us. I mean, really loves us. He does not just offer up words, He is in us through the Holy Spirit and loving us there. He has told us repeatedly in scripture that He loves us with perfect love.

We have the assurance that He has planned our days all out for us and numbered each one. When I don't know what to do or have gotten myself into something I shouldn't have again, I can remind myself that God has the plan. I can look to Him to find where He has for me to be. He can redirect my feet to His path. I am not forever bound to keep wandering under my own direction. He will put my feet back on the straight and narrow if I seek His able help. I just need to ask; He is always ready.

If each of us took moments throughout our days to see where God is and how He is meeting us all along the way, I believe we would live in light of His perspective rather than our own. He longs for us to trust Him for every aspect of our lives.

That thing we think is of no mind to Him might actually be the very thing on His mind. Before we discount His level of interest in our doings, we need to look for His presence and assurance to us.

God did not bring us into this world and leave us here to ourselves. What great news this is! He has done all of the prep work, and He will lead us through it in obvious ways if we are looking at Him. If, however, we are not using the vision that He has given us, then we will certainly overlook many things.

One thing that helped me greatly in this area has been learning to use quiet spaces to think of God present with me. In those fifteen seconds at the stoplight, I think about God. I try to thank Him for something in the immediate. I thank Him for His protection or for the person He let me speak to in the store earlier. I thank Him for the sunshine or for my husband, my best friend.

We have to seek out those moments to find the blessed assurances that are so very important in our days and yet so easily overlooked by us. I believe that we can shift our thinking by what we put in our minds. If we are focused in those moments on God then we are going to know His presence by looking to Him in that quiet.

There will always be an abundance of things to worry about or fret over. But God does not want us to focus on those things; He wants us to focus on Him. If it is so easy to stay focused on the worries, then it is equally easy to focus on God instead. I know that the more I practice using those free moments to think on Him, the more I realize just how many free moments there are in my days. The time is there for us to use, and the choice of how we will spend it is up to us. I have been doing this now for years and my relationship with God has gotten closer and closer. I hope you'll join me today in intentionally seeking God for His blessed assurances. He is waiting.

Dear Father,

Thank You that at any moment we find ourselves in, we can shift our thinking to You and the nearness of Your presence. Teach us, Lord, to seek You throughout the day and find You and the assurances that You give generously to us through Your Word. I want nothing more than to grow closer to You.

Amen.

Colossians 2:5 Psalm 73:23 Psalm 106:1

Blessed Assurances

Genesis 28:15

1. Do you feel the assurance of God's presence with you? Describe.

2. What assurances in the scripture do you find most personal to you? List a few.

3. Do you ask God for reassurances when you doubt or struggle with choices? How has He met you in the past?

4. Where in your daily life can you make spaces to connect with God? How will you accomplish this?

5. What are three verses you can write on sticky notes and put in obvious places to remind yourself to focus on God and His presence with you?

The Great Shepherd

"He will tend his flock like a shepherd; he will gather the lambs in his arms; he will carry them in his bosom, and gently lead those that are with young."

Isaiah 40:11

What do you know about shepherds? Other than what I've read about them, I know very little. Most people know that they tend to sheep and protect them at times from prey and themselves. Many times in scripture we are given the example of God and Christ as a shepherd. This verse comes from way back in Isaiah, which was long before Christ came to be born.

The contexts of these verses are such a tender and personal picture of God to me. First, if we consider sheep and their makeup, we will see that, basically, they are lost without a shepherd. They didn't get a great deal of smarts. They are dependent on one with greater understanding to protect them and care for them.

So, in these verses, I think it's important to see that God didn't choose to lead the most brilliant of His beings as an example to those of us who would come behind. He chose to use the image of a creature that needs lots of guidance and direction. I am definitely that kind of a creature. I have a lot of great ideas, but God far exceeds any of my notions or ideas. He sees me as I really am, and He knows that I am the sheep who needs His shepherding.

I find it easier to walk through this life knowing that I have His leading and guidance. I've sought my own way many times. Those experiences have definitely brought me to the conclusion that I am a needy sheep. The times that I have strayed, I have been the first to know. God has allowed me to wander a bit, but He has always returned me to the fold in His good timing. There was a time in my life when things were difficult, and in my own desperation, I sought out a situation that, in the end, yielded no good. I made excuse upon excuse to God. I even found confidence in my decisions until I realized that when things got quiet, I was all alone. Even God seemed removed.

I have experienced some of the greatest moments in my lifetime, and I have lived in some great moments of loneliness, too. At some point, I began to question my poor decision, but I continued on the path. I was fine in and of myself until my heart got involved, and things got quiet. I had hit a place in life where I thought that God had forgotten me, so I just marched right on by myself. But that piercing quiet destroyed any sense of peace within my being. I could not deny it, but oh, how I tried.

In this verse in Isaiah, we are told that God carries the lambs in His arms and holds them to His bosom. I did not feel God's arms about me nor hear His heart beating within my ear. I had absolutely no doubt that I was not in God's will, and yet I continued to stray, believing that things would get better with time. They did not. In fact, they got worse.

When all my poor decisions crumbled about me, I knew full well why they had done so. I was a dumb sheep and left to my own devices, all I could do was stray. I look back on that time now, so many years later, and realize that I knew that I needed to change direction, but I was unwilling to yield to my Shepherd. Oh, to go back and do it all over again differently. But God, my great shepherd, did not let me continue to stray. He came to me in my ignorance and led me back to the fold. I knew then and now know that I am unworthy of such love.

God can leave each of us where we are and yet if we are called according to His purpose and are His children then we have a hope beyond ourselves. The Shepherd will indeed leave the ninety-nine to come find one lost creature like me, like you.

These verses are so personal as I sit here reading them over. There are lots of days when I feel pretty dumb. I can make myself feel like a failure and God knew I would go there. He gave these verses for me. I need to accept that I need His guidance every moment of every day in order to continue. I don't have what I need, He does. I have to be willing and humble enough to accept my position before Him.

The final part of this verse reflects on how God sees those who are with young. I believe that God has extra grace for mothers of babies. When I think back to having children, I feel pretty sure I knew just how dependent I was on God for that little life. This verse brings us assurance that God takes extra care of us in that stage of life. God has such a tender heart toward us girls. Remind yourself of this truth next time you are beating yourself up for falling into that same weakness again. He knows us, and He gets that we are slow at learning these things. The key comes in when we see that He is tender with us even in those moments of repeated stumbling. His love and leading never waver.

I don't know about you, but that makes me grateful over and over again. It helps me see myself in a greater light of how He sees me. I am humbled that the God of the universe would call me to be His and then understand that I am one slow sheep that is in complete and utter need of His constant guidance and care. Guess what? Every time we stray, He is waiting. Every time, He gathers me back to His arms and pulls me to His bosom so that I can hear the beating of His heart. He cares for me. No matter where you are today, He cares for you in just the same way. Look to the Shepherd and let Him bring clarity to your waywardness and lead you into paths of righteousness.

Father in heaven,

Too many days, I feel the ignorance of my own decisions and the waywardness of my choices. You are always just a heartbeat away from my poor choices and You are waiting for me. I am unworthy, and yet You wait for me. How gracious You are, tender Father. Thank You for loving beyond my wildest imaginings.

Amen.

John 10:11 John 10:14 Matthew 18:13

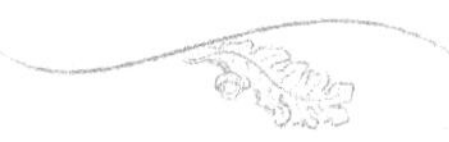

The Great Shepherd
Isaiah 40:11

1. What do you know about shepherds and sheep? Write a few facts about each.

2. How do you identify with being a wandering sheep? How have you strayed and been brought back?

3. Why do you think we are so prone to go our own way? Explain.

4. When you think about the fact that God would leave all of the others to come and get you, how does that make you feel? How much does He love you? Describe.

5. Humility is key to our relationship with the Lord as our Shepherd. How is God calling you to greater humility as His sheep? What will you lay down for the Shepherd?

Acknowledgements

Mary Ward, Coach
coachmaryward@gmail.com
This book would never have come into existence if you had not coached me into process.
Many, many thanks.

Eddie Jones, Writing Coach
You've taught me things that I needed to know to reach that one woman through obedience to Christ. Thank you.
WritersCoach.us@gmail.com

Fanny Crosby, Hymnist
My title comes from your hymn that over the years has inspired me to continue to reach deeper that I might grow nearer to God.

"I am Thine, O Lord, I have heard Thy voice,
And it told Thy love to me,
But I long to rise in the arms of faith,
And be closer drawn to Thee."

Hannah Lender, Cover Designer
www.hannahlinderdesgins.com
You took my words and gave them substance. Your work inspires me. Thank you.

Chloe Giancola, Photographer
www.chloegiancolaphotography.com
You find the best in everything and bring it to light.
Thank you, my younger sister.

www.ingramcontent.com/pod-product-compliance
Lightning Source LLC
LaVergne TN
LVHW020517060425
807795LV00008B/30

9798990493902